The First Principles of Investment
By J. Beattie Crozier

THE FIRST PRINCIPLES OF INVESTMENT

INTRODUCTION

THE distinguished political economists, English and foreign, who, in *The Financial Review of Reviews*, have taken part in the discussion of the question of the "Geographical Distribution of Capital" have, with the single exception perhaps of Mr. Hobson, been adherents of the Old Political Economy of the Schools, and have taken not only their method of approach but the point of view which they have brought with them to the discussion, from its distinctive and peculiar teachings. It is perhaps hardly necessary for me to say here that all the fundamental principles and tenets of this Old Economy of Adam Smith and Stuart Mill have Free Trade as their logical sequence and corollary; or, to repeat what I have so often had occasion to point out elsewhere, that they all end in the belief that whatever benefits trade in any one country *necessarily* benefits it in each and every other with which that country has international business dealings.

Now, this latter proposition I venture to unhesitatingly deny, and to affirm, on the contrary, that under a universal Free Trade between nations it will only the more certainly be found that an increase of wealth founded on the supremacy of a particular trade in any one country is sure to be followed by a corresponding decline in the same trade in all those other countries which up to then had, by natural or artificial Protection, become rich and powerful by its exercise.

This is a proposition to which universal history, mocking the delusions and hopes of the Old Economists, has in every age of the world borne witness; but at no period perhaps has it focussed itself with so much clearness and pregnancy as in the case of the Hanse towns and of Holland on the ruins of the mercantile trade of Genoa and Venice which followed directly on the discovery of the new Cape route to the East; or of England, in turn, on that of Holland. But it is a proposition as true of manufacturing countries engaged in an international rivalry with the same class of goods as it is in the mercantile and shipping trades. Sooner or later under a universal Free Trade they must come to a hand-to-hand grapple with each other, and the quicker the more free is the trade between them; and then, as in all human things, the strongest will carry off the prize. There is no sharing and sharing alike between the conquerors and the conquered anywhere or in any concern in this world.

But all this is, indeed, only the natural and necessary deduction from the principles of the New Economy which, in this discussion, I am now to apply to the problem of the Geographical Distribution of Capital, and which I have set forth with a sufficiency of detail in my *Wheel of Wealth*. Or, to put it differently, a policy of Protection for nations in the present industrial development of the world follows as naturally and by as rigid a logical sequence from the principles of the New Economy as a policy of Free Trade followed from the opposite principles of the Old Economy; but with this advantage in favour of the New Economy, that it is founded throughout on maxims which every business man recognises, believes in, and acts upon, and not on false abstractions like that of the "economic man" of the Old Economy, or (especially in this age of Trusts, Combines, and Tariffs), on the delusive imagination of an "absolutely free competition," or the now played-out role of *laissez-faire*—all of which business men have long since thrown on the dead scrap-heap as quite useless either for their instruction or profit.

It is a fine piece of pedantry on the part of the Old Economists that, having founded their system on the industrial regime of a particular nation—and that, too, covering a period of not more than fifty years in all its history—they should still continue airily and complacently to keep it going on the same principles of that regime, under the pretence that they would allow for the exceptional instances where Trusts, Combinations, Monopolies, and Tariffs have taken the place of the "economic man," free competition, and laissez-faire; and of the instances where the industrial or money powers of individuals, classes, or nations have, like highwaymen, held up other individuals, classes, or nations, while they appropriated to themselves the spoils. As if, indeed, there ever was a time in the history of the world (even in the short reign of industrial Free Trade and Free Contract) when some individuals, or classes, or nations, had not by their power managed either to enslave outright, to reduce to serfdom, or to industrially exploit the rest, from the time of the dominion of the sword in the ancient and mediaeval world to that of the dominion of the dollar, as in the American Trusts of to-day. They might as well, like the old anatomists, start from the dissection of the dead body, and then allow for the laws of its physiology when alive, instead of starting from the living, and allowing for its manifestations when dead.

And I appeal to the reader whether it is not time that Political Economy should start afresh from the living industrial facts of to-day— Trusts, Combination, Monopoly, Co-operation, and the incidence of personal or money power, all of which have come to stay—and only then allow for the effects of Free Competition, Freedom of Contract, and *laissez-faire*, when these still linger on around the outskirts or in the shade. And I take it as a step in this direction, and as a recognition of the rapidity with which the New Economy is making its way, as well as an indication of the freedom from bias which the Editor of *The Financial Review of Reviews* has shown in desiring to have all schools of economic thought represented in his pages, that I should have been invited to set forth the principles of the New Economy in their bearings on this important and practical problem of the Geographical Distribution of Capital.

What, then, are the points of this problem on which Political Economy is invited to pass judgment? The problem itself may be stated in a word, namely, how to get out of investments the greatest amount of income compatible with the absolute safety of the capital invested. And the questions which the Editor wants answered from the standpoint of adherents both of the Old and the New Economy are: 1st, What effect will the Geographical Distribution of Capital have on individual investors; 2nd, What on the nation to which these investors happen to belong; and 3rd, What on the world of international trade and industry as a whole?

Now, it is to the security and welfare of the individual investor under this scheme that the greater part of the following pages' will be devoted; but I may say here in a general way that I do not think that on this point there can be two opinions. In my judgment, Mr. Henry Lowenfeld, the author and originator of this scheme of Geographical Distribution, has, as we shall see in detail later, reduced it to something like a scientific demonstration, when regard is had, that is to say, to the ticklish risks which attend every investment of capital in a world so rapid-changing and everywhere subject to so many unforeseeable industrial and financial contingencies and cataclysms. And, in passing, I may be permitted here to congratulate him on the wonderful unanimity with which his scheme has been everywhere received by financial experts of every kind: bankers, brokers, officials of the Chambers of Commerce, foreign financial authorities, etc., as well as by the most eminent political economists, English and foreign, of the old Academic School. To this unanimity of opinion from the adherents of the Old Economy I am willing to subscribe for what it is worth my own tribute of appreciation from the point of view of the New.

To many, if not most readers, perhaps the phrase "Geographical Distribution of Capital'" would suggest that the scheme is only a variant on the old general injunction that if you wish to sleep o' nights you ought not to put all your eggs into one basket. But this kind of security can, as regards capital safety, be had almost haphazard, as out of a bag, by any one who will select a sufficient number of gilt-edged securities from out of the ordinary miscellaneous assortment of them on the market. And yet, when we remember that Consols even, with their low rate of interest, would, during the last ten or more years, have lost the investor quite a fourth of his capital were he obliged to sell them out to-day, it is obvious that even the most gilt-edged securities cannot be depended on even as regards the safety of the capital invested in them. But when an increase of income over and above that of the humble yield from Consols or other first-class stocks of the same character is desired, then this easy method of putting all your eggs into these various gilt-edged baskets is quite out of the question. No! Mr. Lowenfeld's scheme, although, it is true, a question of baskets, is not one of this simple and easy kind; but, on the contrary, is a scientific statement of precisely what quality, kind, and location of basket you are to put your eggs into; and, like all scientific generalisations which are of ultimate value, is founded on what I believe is admitted to be perhaps the largest and most carefully sifted collection of stocks and shares from all the world yet known, and includes their past history as well as their present status; all of them being brought together month after month in the pages of *The Financial Review of Reviews.*

Later on, I shall put the whole scheme, with its appendages and abutments, on to the world-wheel of wealth production and distribution which symbolises the method of the New Economy, to see how it will turn out. But in the meantime I can personally re-echo the opinion of Professor Karl Brämer, as expressed in a recent number of the Review, that "Mr. Lowenfeld's book develops the principles of a new science— Comparative Trade Statistics—formerly treated as a side branch of statistics; but now it can claim to be a special science of itself"; or of Mr. Hobson, who says that "Lowenfeld has shown that profit varies directly and risk inversely with Geographical Distribution, which gives the largest, safest, and most equable dividends." It will be interesting, therefore, to see how this scheme in its international, national, and individual aspects works out under analysis.

CHAPTER I.ON THE NATURAL VALUE OF DIFFERENT STOCKS: BANKS AND INSURANCE COMPANIES

IT is an indispensable preliminary to any really scientific estimate of the value of the principle of the Geographical Distribution of Capital, as a mode of investment, that we should at the outset ascertain what we may call the *natural* value of the different classes of securities on the market, with the view of determining the order in which, like geological strata, they lie one above another in the financial hierarchy. For just as it is necessary to know the natural order of the rocks composing the earth's crust before we can understand the topsy-turvy inversions and dislocations which local upheavals and depressions have here and there produced among them, so it is necessary to know the natural order and rank of the credit values of different species of stock if we are to take advantage of those inversions of their natural order which are always occurring in some of the countries of the world, where, like an inverted pyramid, stocks naturally highest in the scale are found lying far down towards the bottom, and those naturally at the bottom high up towards the top. Indeed, as we shall see farther on, it is on these inversions and dislocations, and on a knowledge of the causes which give rise to them, and, therefore, on the advantage that can be taken of that knowledge, that the principle of the Geographical Distribution of Capital gets its foothold and justification.

I am aware, of course, that there is no such thing as a purely *natural* value adhering to any particular stock or piece of property whatever; for all, of course, depend on circumstances and conditions, on supply and demand, and the rest. What I wish the reader to understand by the *natural* value of a stock is the value which attaches not to any particular stock as such, but to the *class* of securities to which it belongs, whether this value be due to the possession of certain *positive* natural advantages, or negatively to the freedom from certain natural risks, or both.

As a rule, the natural value of a stock includes both advantages and risks; but it will be found that while some stocks get their rank mainly from their advantages, others get it mainly from their absence of risk. It is only when the two are taken together and a balance struck between them that the difference in natural value or rank of the stock, whether as higher, lower, or on an even level with other classes of stocks, can be said to be determined; as, for example, between Government stocks and Banking, Banking and Insurance companies; between these again and Corporation Loans or Railway Debentures, and between all these and the ordinary shares of industrial and commercial enterprise. But to ascertain this it is necessary to reduce them all alike, if possible, to some common denominator as it were, by passing them through a number of generalised categories which shall sum up their main characteristics, both of advantages and risks. They may be classified as follows:

1. The extent, mass, permanence, and stability of the securities on which they rest.

2. The extent to which they rest primarily on Money and its range of fluctuations, and only secondarily on Industry; or primarily on Industry and its range of fluctuations, and only secondarily on Money.

3. The extent to which they rest on such previsions as are possible in the ups and downs of industrial business of all kinds on the one hand; or on calculations that fall under the mathematical Laws of Probability on the other.

4. The extent to which the element of Time enters into the composition of their business bargains.

5. The amount of natural Monopoly that attaches to them from peculiarities of their situation or surroundings, or owing to the mass of

free Capital which they can concentrate on any business situation at any moment.

The above have direct reference to the positive advantages of different classes of stock. But these once ascertained, we have still to turn the stocks over on to their negative or reverse side, as it were, for the purpose of ascertaining the extent, magnitude, and imminence of the risks to which they are exposed. These comprise:

1. The extent to which the risks are sudden and incalculable, or so foreseeable as to enable investors to prepare against them either wholly or in part. An altogether incalculable risk is, of course, a pure gamble, and not a proper subject for scientific investment, unless, indeed, it can be controlled by the mathematical Law of Probabilities.

2. The extent to which Politics and other outside complications interfere with different classes of stock, and make their possession, as a permanent source of investment, precarious.

3. The extent to which the condition of the Money Market in the different countries or the particular Money Market in which stocks of different countries are mainly dealt in, affects the relative value of stocks of the same class in these different countries by imparting to them either activity or stagnation.

Now, as we shall see farther on, it is to the intrusion of Politics on the one hand, and of the condition of the Money Markets of the world on the other, that are chiefly due those dislocations and inversions of the natural value of stocks on which, as Mr. Lowenfeld was the first to point out, the principle of the Geographical Distribution of Capital depends for the success of its operations. Let us then pass the different classes of stocks through the categories I have just enumerated, with the view of seeing how their natural values as securities will turn out in relation to each other when they are passed through this mill and reduced to common denominators.

The first category we have mentioned, namely, the extent, mass, permanence, and stability of the securities on which any class of stocks rests, is, in spite of its being the most generalised and vague, the most important of all in so far as the natural value of a stock is concerned. It is what gives Consols, and the stocks of the different Governments of the world, their position at the head of all other stocks whatever of the same country; and that for the simple reason that they are secured on the entire resources of a nation, whereas all other loans—except those with a definite Government guarantee—are secured both on a lesser amount and on a narrower range of resources, as in the case of Corporation Loans, which are secured only on the property of particular cities or towns, or of Joint Stock Companies and other ordinary business loans, on the property of a limited number of individuals only—the proprietors.

Now, if this be the case, the reader may object that if an ideal safety be an investor's aim, all he would have to do would be to distribute his capital among the Government stocks of the best accredited nations, and his problem would be solved. Yes; were it not for certain important reservations and qualifications. But it must be remembered that Government stocks, by reason of their position at the head of all other stocks in their own country, yield the lowest rate of interest; and something more than that is what the investor wants. The ideal safety of his capital is not, in a word, the only object the prudent investor has in view. His problem, on the contrary, is rather a triple-sided one, namely, how to get the greatest yield of interest for his money compatible with the greatest practical security and stability, not the greatest *ideal* or ultimate security. In other words, he balances the ideal security of Government stocks against their low yield of interest; and, if he can get practical security and stability with larger yield, he will take the chances, as is now done by trustees.

And it is precisely this larger yield with equal practical security which the Geographical Distribution of Capital professes to insure to those who follow its teachings. How it is done, and how stocks, which, although possessing less ideal safety, perhaps, than Government stocks, can yet be held with as much practical safety, and often, eventually possessing greater uniformity and stability, can only be fully seen when we have ascertained the natural value and rank of the other great classes of securities outside Government stocks. And this we shall be able to do by applying to them the other categories I have laid down.

It will be expedient, perhaps, to consider the next three categories together: firstly, the extent to which a class of securities gets rank by resting throughout primarily on Money rather than on Industry; secondly, the extent to which it gets rank from resting on the mathematical Law of Probabilities rather than on such prevision as is possible in the ups and downs of industry and trade; and thirdly, the part which the *element of time* plays in raising or lowering the rank of any class of stock, into which it enters as a leading factor. Now, the stocks which get their rank from the parts played in them by these distinctive features are mainly those of Banks and Insurance Companies, and to those I would now direct the reader's attention somewhat in detail.

To begin with, there are various reasons why all such stocks as rest throughout primarily on Money have the advantage over all stocks that rest primarily on the ups and downs of business and trade. The first is that Money is itself the final term in every business transaction, the commodity into which all other commodities and credit values must be reduced before the wealth contained in them can be estimated or realised. Like Jupiter among the lesser gods, it coerces all other commodities and values into terms of itself; and hence it is that, whereas all other commodities after a business deal come out either enlarged or shrunk in value through the ups and downs of markets and the process of sale, Money, like a billiard ball, comes out precisely of the same value as it went in; and, as it can never want for customers, stocks that rest on money throughout have a natural security, stability, and freedom from risk which are not to be found in industrial and commercial commodities, which have to run the gauntlet of sale and the finding of a customer before they can be turned into money.

Again, being itself the standard of value as well as its measure, Money is the commodity which varies least over great lapses of time, while over short periods, when compared with all other commodities, it may well stand as the image and type of stability itself. It neither deteriorates appreciably by wear and tear, as other commodities do, nor at all by keeping; nor is its value affected, as with other commodities, by new inventions and processes; nor does it depend for its stability on the genius, foresight, skill, or life of its owners; and so it can be more depended on to keep its own proper value intact over the ordinary periods during which business transactions run, than any other commodity whatever. And accordingly, businesses resting throughout primarily on Money as their stock in trade, both of purchase and sale, take a natural rank for stability and security of investment, as well as for freedom from risk of loss of capital, far above what is attainable in the wide fluctuations of market values and the constant ups and downs which characterise the business transactions which rest primarily on Industry and Trade. It is true, of course, that Money, like the sun in its relative position among the planets and stars, slowly changes its value in reference to other commodities over long periods of time, but over short periods the change is so slight as to be practically inappreciable. But if, besides resting primarily on Money, a business rests also on the mathematical Law of Probabilities, it will take an even higher rank for stability than if it rested on Money alone; for the possessor will not only be able to equalise the risks that arise amid the multiplicity of individual transactions which make up his business, so that he will get back sovereigns for sovereigns, but also to make sure of an even profit as well. And, further still, if a business rests on transactions in which the element of time is so short that they are as near to cash transactions as possible, it will have attained to the highest natural rank of investment for stability, security, and freedom from risk.

Now, the ideal of a combination such as I have described, where a pure Money business rests on the Law of Probabilities, and confines its transactions to cash payments only, is best seen in such an institution as the gaming Bank of Monte Carlo; and it may well be taken as a standard by which all stocks which rest primarily on this basis, although not in such ideal form, may be measured. For not only its capital and reserve, but all its transactions are in money down, with no process of bargain and sale to disturb calculations, nor ups and downs of supply and demand, nor conditions of Money Markets, no estimates of the credits of customers, no intrusions of outside or business complication; while all risks from the chances of individual spins or runs of luck are neutralised by the operation of the Law of Probabilities, which, working under ideal conditions in the construction of the tables, grinds out its level profit in cash with undeviating regularity. In other words, while the previsions and calculations, on which all ordinary businesses depend for success, must always be a matter of more or less uncertain speculation, and of hit or miss, the Bank of Monte Carlo, like a piece of artillery mounted and planted on a level plain, can be so sighted and adjusted by means of the zero and the limitation of stakes, as to hit its mark—the share of profit it proposes to take for itself— every time; and the longer the wheel continues to spin, the more exactly will the profits of the table correspond to the amount allotted to it beforehand by the application to it of the Law of Probabilities, and with nothing to limit the yield of these profits but the number of customers who can be induced to patronise the bank in a given period of time. In this way it defies, in its freedom from risks, the mutations of ordinary business, as the Pyramids defy the mutations of time.

Now, with the Bank of Monte Carlo as our ideal and standard for estimating the status of all stocks resting primarily on the triple pillars of Money, the Law of Probabilities, and Cash Payment, we may next proceed to try to estimate the relative status, as safe and stable investments, of Banking and Insurance companies respectively, both of which rest mainly on the same triple pillars, but are prevented from reaching this ideal security by the admixture in each, in varying degrees and proportions, of the risks pertaining to ordinary industrial and commercial businesses.

Let us then begin with banks. Like the Bank of Monte Carlo, they rest throughout primarily on money, or on such securities for money as cheques, which, although not legal tender, and, like railway tickets, good only for a single transaction, can nevertheless perform all the functions of money with a minimum of risk. Like the Bank of Monte Carlo, too, ordinary banking relies on the action of the Law of Probabilities for the stability and security of its profits; for it is only on the probability that the cash drawn out of the bank by cheques and discounts at one counter will be replaced by a continuous return of different cheques and deposits at another, that the outgoings and incomings of the bank can be counted upon to keep in a moving equilibrium with each other. Indeed, without this antecedent probability it would be impossible for a bank (with its legal compulsion to meet its notes and floating deposits in cash on demand) to estimate the amount of reserve in cash necessary to keep on hand, or, indeed, to do business on borrowed capital at all.

Again, the capital investments of banks are lent only on such securities as can be turned into cash at the shortest notice, and so the bank keeps as closely to the ideal security of Monte Carlo as is possible. Where it falls short is in the necessity, under which it lies, of having collateral as security at all, instead of cash. For on any hitch occurring, this collateral, however gilt-edged it may be, has to be sold, and so is subject to the state of the Money Market at the time, and to the fluctuations of Stock Exchange securities generally. And although this would not be any very great detriment, provided the collateral were sufficient to amply cover the debt, and there was time enough to realise it in, it is always a danger, where liabilities have to be met, as in banking, by cash on demand on pain of bankruptcy. Indeed, if we turn the banking business over on its reverse side to see what its natural risks are, we shall find that this is essentially its only risk, just as when an army has its lines extended so far from any given point of attack that it cannot bring up its full strength in time.

The Panic, which descends so suddenly out of the clouds, and leaves so much desolation behind it, and which is the form that this risk of not keeping time usually takes, is not in itself a natural risk in banking, in the sense, that is to say, that it is either inherent in the ordinary rules of the game, or due, as most other business risks are, to the impossibility of absolute foresight into the state of markets and prices in the future. These panics are due rather to the bad faith and unscrupulousness of directors or managers on the one hand, or to their excess of optimism or good nature in making advances to their customers on insufficient or improper collateral on the other—not to the want of capacity to master the few plain rules which are sufficient to enable any honest and sensible man to avoid either the immediate or the predisposing cause of these terrible visitations. Indeed, so strongly is the credit of banking naturally entrenched in its basis at once of Money, of the operation of the Law of Probabilities, and of the most easily realisable substitutes for Cash itself, that it only requires the most ordinary prudence and honesty to reduce everywhere the danger from panics to the minimum negligible point, which it has reached in England to-day. Now, taking all these considerations together, it will be evident that banks have as easy and automatic an action, as high a natural rank as stable and safe investments, as is possible perhaps outside the ideal of the Bank of Monte Carlo. Further peculiarities bearing on their natural rank and risks will appear when we contrast them with insurance companies, as I now propose to do.

To begin with, we may say generally that Insurance companies, although, like banks, they rest primarily on Money and the operation of the Law of Probabilities, do not lie as closely to a cash basis at all points as banks, and so participate more largely in the risks inseparable from long-time as compared with short-time investments. They would seem, therefore, at first sight to have a less natural stability and freedom from risk than Bank stock; but whether this superior position may not be reversed in the future will depend upon considerations at which we shall now have to glance in passing. Both banks and insurance companies rest primarily, as we have said, on money, and upon their transactions in it—the banks on their capital deposits received from the public, the insurance companies on their capital and the premiums received from their policy holders. In both, again, their returns come back directly in money, and not in merchandise which still has to run the uncertain risks of sale before it is converted into money. But while with banks the mathematical Law of Probabilities is so smooth and even in its working—owing to the short circuit of each transaction— that the deposits and discounts, on which the profits of the bank so largely depend, come in in equable and regular file, in insurance companies, on the other hand, the Law of Probabilities has to work through statistics and tables of chances, which, although they are always being improved and provided against, are still far from reliable. And the consequence of this is, that, while in the ordinary way of business the proportion of cash which the bank must keep by it as its reserve can be easily estimated, and can be depended upon to remain steady throughout, if the rules of prudence proper to banking are observed, in insurance companies, especially in cases of fire, the risks come rolling in for payment intermittently, like epidemics, and so require not only a larger proportional reserve to meet them, but one which demands more careful watching, if it is to keep time and proportion with the risks. So far, then, the risks not being so calculable, they are not so safe as banks. But as a set-off, the insurance companies, so far as the future is concerned, have this advantage, that whereas the risks of the banks are neither diminished nor increased by the extent of their operations or the circle of their clientele, inasmuch as the extent of their business does not affect either way the periodicity and accuracy of their incomings and outgoings, the risks of insurance companies must diminish as the field covered by their policies increases in magnitude and range; so much so, indeed, that were a single insurance company to embrace the world, its risks could be taken haphazard for all comers without inspection, or, in the case of lives, medical examination, inasmuch as the Law of Probabilities working on the statistics of the death rates of all nations would enable the average of profits to be calculated to almost a working certainty.

And the question arises whether banks have any set-off in the future which will balance this progressive advantage on the side of the insurance companies. Yes, if the probability of a higher moral standard in the management and administration of banks in the future may be relied on to lessen the risks of panics. All the foremost nations of the world become, as time goes on, more sensitive and morally responsive to the necessity of keeping their assets in such securities only as can be converted into money on the shortest notice, as well as making their advances to customers only on such collateral as can be so converted, besides being sufficient in amount. In this way the danger from panics, which rarely arise except from suspicion of carelessness or unscrupulousness, would be reduced to a minimum or altogether averted; whereas, in insurance companies neither honesty nor industry will probably ever avail to anticipate or prevent destructive fires like those of San Francisco or Messina. These could, of course, be provided against in a measure by special reserves set aside for the purpose, or by greater combinations and sharings of risks among the different companies; but all this adds to cost, and so far throws back the advantage in yield, as well as in stability, on to the side of the banks again. It would seem as if panics lay, as it were, outside the circuit of a bank's natural risks, and were rather a matter of personal prudence and character in the administration of them than inherent in their essence; whereas in insurance companies, especially those providing against accidents from fire or flood or storm, the risks are inherent, natural, and proper to the business itself.

Again, the investments of Banks are either in gilt-edged securities, the most easily convertible into cash, or in those which run their course in such short periods of time that they can scarcely in the intervals of renewals, with their various endorsements or acceptances, get far out of hand without detection and the prevention of loss; whereas in the long-time investments of Insurance Companies, the directors may be condemned to stand and look on while their securities slowly become worthless. It is true there are possibilities of gain in the longtime investments of the Insurance Companies which are not open to Banks doing a legitimate business, and which are confronted with the dangers of panic on any failure to meet their deposits on demand; and these may well reverse the relative status of the Insurance Companies and the Banks, inasmuch as they will not only command a greater yield of income, but one which in the future may be expected to rest on a basis of equal stability and security. This, I believe, will eventually be the case if the principle of the Geographical Distribution of Capital, which this publication is intended to support, can be worked out into a true scientific demonstration. Any risks which investments on this principle may run, when compared with the gilt-edged securities of the bankers' operations, would be balanced by the advantages possessed by the Insurance Companies in the length of time given them to negotiate the sale of their securities to the best advantage. The element of time enters into the relative status of Banks and Insurance Companies in other ways, but mainly through the effects of the Money Market on profits and stability.

The profits of Banks vary with the fluctuations of the Bank rate; when the Bank rate is low, and money in consequence is cheaper, the yield is less than when it stands at medium rate between high and low. Provided that the state of trade and business in general remains steady, a high Bank rate restricts the demand for bank accommodation, although the profits of the bank are high on each transaction. A low rate, on the other hand, stimulates the demand, but the profits in each transaction are small; it is the medium, or average, rate which gives, perhaps, the most satisfactory returns. On Insurance Companies, on the other hand, with their investments resting largely on long-time engagements, and with no pressing necessity of payment on demand, the temporary fluctuations of the Money Market have less influence. It is only long-time or permanent changes in the value of money that can have much influence on the yield from their investments, and this can be largely neutralised and averaged, as we shall see later, by a geographical distribution among the Money Markets of different nations; and then the yield from the Insurance Companies' investments would be larger than those from the Banks.

Indeed, it is questionable whether the yield from the Insurance Companies, by their skilful handling of these investments, may not prove in time as steady, safe, and stable a revenue as from their insurance business proper. It ought at least to form a reserve for the greater calamities to which they are subject. A drawback to the advantages of any scheme of investment lies in the fact that their securities, in the event of any great drafts being made on them suddenly, or on their term having run out, are liable to forced sales on unpropitious markets and to the difficulty of finding at the moment other investments equally good to replace them; but this difficulty a geographical distribution may be trusted to reduce to a minimum. As to the risks, which appertain both to Banks and Insurance Companies from unpaid-up Capital, terrible as these risks are, and common as is the practice of our English Banks and Insurance Companies in running them, they may be said to be incidental rather to the proper business of these concerns than natural risks inherent in them, and could be altered by legislation to-morrow.

To sum up, then, these various considerations of relative advantages and risks, we may say, perhaps, that up to the present day Banks have a higher natural safety, stability, and yield, than Insurance Companies, owing to the greater closeness with which they lie to their money basis at every stage of their transactions, to the greater reliability with which the Law of Probabilities can be applied to them, and to the shorter time in which their cash assets are out of their immediate tangible possession. But in spite of all this, it is still an open question whether in the future the freedom which Insurance Companies enjoy in the range and choice of their investments, but which is denied to the Banks, may not result in incomes from that source alone so much larger than those of the Banks (and, under the auspices of the new science of the Geographical Distribution of Capital, equally safe) as to form a second line of reserve, as it were, which will more than cover the greater unavoidable risks to which the Insurance Companies must always be exposed. But if this be not enough to transfer the balance of advantage to the Insurance Companies, it will probably be made up by the lessening of risk due to the greater field covered by them in the future, to their greater combination for the sharing of risks, and to the progressive perfecting of the tables of chances on which the Law of Probabilities will be able to work. From all of which complication of considerations, the reader will see how difficult it is to determine scientifically the relative status for the future of Banks and Insurance Companies respectively. At the present time it is probable that Banks, in Great Britain at least, are the more steady, safe, and reliable investments of the two.

CHAPTER II.ON THE NATURAL VALUE OF DIFFERENT CLASSES OF SECURITIES—INDUSTRIAL MONOPOLIES

IN the present chapter I propose to begin by considering the natural value of those stocks which rest primarily on Industrial Monopoly, complete or partial (and not, like Banks and Insurance Companies, on Money) as a preliminary to that large class of securities which, like Corporation Loans, Railway and other Debentures, rest on a combination of all three—Industry, Monopoly, and Money. As to all ordinary industrial stocks, such as are represented by the Ordinary shares of a Joint Stock Company, they are so subject to all the ups and downs of market prices, of brisk and slack trade, of "goodwill" or the loss of "goodwill," of new inventions, new machinery, new chemical processes, and what not, that the incomes from them, however great they may chance to be, are as uncertain and fluctuating as the rocking foundations on which they rest. In a word, they are as a class the subject-matter of speculation and chance, and not of scientific generalisation and prevision; and their natural rank, in consequence, when compared with investments resting on Money, is as much lower in the scale as the gambling of the outside public on the turf is than that of the scientific bookmakers, or that of the players at the Bank of Monte Carlo than that of the bank itself.

Indeed, from their natural want of stability and security, the Ordinary shares of Joint Stock Companies may be said to stand at the bottom of the scale of investments. Not that there may not be Golcondas among them, or that the majority of them may not be steady-going concerns yielding average dividends, even if there be a large minority that are virtually bankrupt or on the verge of it; and doubtless to the promoters, who have inner knowledge of these concerns, it is often, though not always, sufficiently well known under which of these categories their own particular stock will fall. But this cannot be known to the outside general public, nor, as we shall see later on, will the published audit of the accounts of these companies by the methods of bookkeeping in vogue reveal it to them—except to the few who know how to read between the lines.

Now, all this is reversed in the case of those industries that have managed to convert themselves into Monopolies. For then, instead of being the hangers-on of business chance and fortune, they are able in a measure to defy them; and their stocks have, in consequence, a natural value on a level with those stocks which rest, like Banks and Insurance Companies, on Money and the mathematical Law of Probabilities—and indeed above them, if the monopoly be a complete one, as we shall presently see. For both the stocks that rest on Money and those that rest on Monopoly get their high rank from the power they have of controlling the selling end of their bargains as it were, and of keeping it in correspondence with the buying or cost end. Banks get this power through the quality which money possesses (owing to its being the standard and measure of value) of being practically *equal* value at both ends of the usually short-time loan transactions in which they deal; and by the Law of Probabilities which, as we saw in the last chapter, keeps a fairly average level of profit throughout. Industrial Monopolies, on the other hand, when they are *complete* ones, get their steadiness and equability by the power of moving their selling price up and down at a fixed percentage of profit, in correspondence with the variations in their buying price or costs.

So far, Banks and Industrial Monopolies are on an equality as far as their stability and security are concerned. But the industrial monopolies have this advantage over Banks and Insurance Companies, which rest on Money and depend on the working of the Law of Probabilities to keep them steady, viz., that whereas the Banks and Insurance Companies have no inherent or natural power of drawing away the customers of other banks of equal capital, honesty, or repute, Industrial Monopolies, when complete, have by their very nature the capacity of absorbing the customers of all lesser concerns by the power they have of underselling them in the open market.

There are many reasons why they have this power. In the first place, they all have some *differential advantages* in their favour which enable them to produce more cheaply than the rest of their competitors in the same line of business. It may be a new invention, a better process or machine, which is sufficient to give them the lead in the trade before the patent runs out; and this lead may afterwards be continued by "goodwill," "trade marks," advertisements, and other extraneous influences. But at the present day, with patent rights so short-lived as they are, this is not sufficient to establish a complete monopoly. There must be some natural advantage in the climate, soil, or water of the region in which the monopoly takes its rise over those of other regions— as is found in the case of certain select brands or descriptions of tobacco, of wine, of ale, or fruit, certain indispensables for high-class cutlery or cotton manufacture, the existence of oil wells, diamond mines, and the like.

Or, again, a Monopoly may take its rise and get its hold from its purely site value as a trading centre, and this whether in the case of an individual trader, a city, or a nation—as is seen in the historical instances of Constantinople, Venice, Amsterdam, and London, and of Spain, Holland, and England generally. But once securely entrenched by these or other means, the monopoly may afterwards maintain itself indefinitely and make itself absolute, by the mere possession of an amount of free capital sufficient when concentrated on any given point to annihilate its rivals by underselling them—as in the case of the Standard Oil, Beef, Sugar, Soap, and other American Trusts. This it can do either directly by buying them out, or by drawing them into amalgamation with itself; or eventually by the power which the enormous aggregation of capital in single hands gives its possessor of keeping down costs below the level of his rivals through the advantages he gets in higher rates of discount, or greater rebates in transportation; in the power his free capital gives him of buying up the best patents and processes, the best talents and services; and, we may add, in the power it gives him of corrupting Courts of Justice in countries where corruption has become a recognised business transaction.

But however strongly a Monopoly may be able to entrench itself by these or other means, it is rarely that it can make itself complete. To do so, it must have the power of controlling its selling end as well as its cost or buying end; and this is scarcely possible, except when it deals in one or other of the great necessaries of life—as is the case with the great American Trusts. But should it succeed in thus controlling its selling end, as well as sealing up its buying end against all attack, it is evident that it will not only be as stable, secure, and equable as the Banks, but that it will have possibilities within it of a much greater yield of income on an equal amount of capital; and so will stand higher in the scale of securities than either Banks or Insurance Companies. For, dealing with those ultimate necessaries which all must buy, and not with such comparative luxuries as are involved in the ability to keep a bank account, or to insure your life or your house, it can never want for customers; nor, indeed, can it if it deals in those collaterals like steel, iron, and timber, which are everywhere involved in production and transportation. Banks and Insurance Companies have a narrower range of customers than these giant Industrial Monopolies, and, being subject to competition among themselves, a lower rate of profit; and so have not only a lower yield on the same amount of capital, but, in consequence, a lower natural rank in the financial scale for stability and security as well.

Incomplete or Partial Monopolies, on the other hand, stand lower in the scale than Banks or Insurance Companies, inasmuch as, however much they may be able to control their cost end, they are unable as a rule to control their selling end, even when there is no alternative commodity on which their customers can fall back as a substitute. A Diamond Monopoly, for example, even were it absolutely secure against competition, could never fix its sale price with the certainty with which a Standard Oil, Meat, Sugar, or Soap Trust, all of which deal with the necessaries of life, can, inasmuch as, being a luxury, the sale of diamonds falls off of itself in periods of crisis or trade stagnation. And although the sales are almost sure to recover when trade revives, this monopoly, even were it complete in its way, cannot have the calculable stability of monopolies founded on the necessaries of life; and so takes a lower rank in the scale of stable, secure, and high-yielding investments. Indeed, Industrial Monopolies which can in any sense be called complete, that is to say, which can control both the buying and the selling ends of their transactions, are, as I have said, the rarest of phenomena.

The land of a country is spoken of as a monopoly, owing to its scarcity; but there are few countries that could control the selling price of their own corn without Protection. As for the ordinary Industrial Monopolies which do not depend on scarcity values, they will have to be internationalised—as, indeed, some of them are fast becoming—before they can so far control their selling ends as to become complete. But for the great mass of Industrial Monopolies there are so many alternatives to the use of any but the most pressing necessaries of life, and so many difficulties in the way of effective "cornering," that they may safely be put under the category of Incomplete or Partial Monopolies, with a status for stability and security lower than Banks and Insurance Companies—to which indeed they stand in the same relation of inferiority as Ordinary Joint Stock shares do to them.

Now these Incomplete or Partial Monopolies may be divided into two classes: those of a private and those of a semi-public character; but they all have this characteristic, that it is only one of their limbs, as it were, on which they can march with safety, the other being shaky and insecure. In semi-public monopolies, as we shall see in the next chapter, some have their selling prices guaranteed to them, but not the cost price or the number of their customers; others have both a given number of customers and a given price, but not the cost; and others again, although guaranteed against competition, have no guarantee for their "turnover" or sales. In private incomplete monopolies, on the other hand, it is the buying or cost leg that is reliable and steady, owing to the possession of *natural* advantages of production which keep down competition; while the selling one, unless protected by tariff, is weak and insecure, owing to the difficulty of controlling prices in the face of foreign competition, or of controlling sales in the face of alternative substitutes.

In this connection it is perhaps interesting to note that no man was more alive to the necessity of controlling the selling as well as the buying end of a commodity, if a monopoly were to be secured, than the late Mr. Rogers of the Standard Oil Trust. In one of his numerous altercations with Mr. Lawson, as recorded in *Frenzied Finance*, he insisted that economists must be taught the lesson that it was essential to a complete monopoly that it should be able to control its sale end as well as its supply end or cost; that it should not only have full control over the raw material and its various processes of manufacture (either by owning them or being able to put sufficient pressure on those who did), but have full control over all the agents and intermediaries engaged in its sale. It was a question of the sale of copper, if I remember rightly, and Mr. Rogers proposed that sufficient pressure should be put on some rival selling agents with the view of crushing them and driving them from the field if in their sales of copper they should refuse to hold up their prices to the level which he dictated. To Mr. Lawson, himself a great operator, all this seemed to come as a revelation—if one may judge from the ecstasies of admiration into which, in his recital and commentary on the affair, he fell over the genius of Mr. Rogers—but I could not help feeling that it must have been the old Academical Economists whom Mr. Rogers had in his eye when he uttered his gibe; for precisely the same principle was involved in every doctrine of the New Economy which I had embodied in my *Wheel of Wealth*.

Now, it is to be observed that in all these incomplete monopolies, where either the buying or the selling end is so unstable that the two cannot be brought together and adjusted so as to form that closed circuit at which Mr. Rogers aimed, no definite rank can be assigned to the particular stock in the hierarchy of stocks at once stable and safe, but each must "hang by its own head," as it were, and stand on its own particular merits alone. To get at the rank of each, we have to look not only for its positive merits, but for the special risks to which it is liable. Some positive merits, one would think, all monopolies, complete or incomplete, must have, or they could not have got the start which has given them their supremacy; but, strangely enough, inherent merits are more likely to be found in incomplete monopolies than in practically complete ones where both ends are controlled, like Standard Oil; inasmuch as the stock-in-trade of the latter being imposed by compulsion and not by preference, may, like dirty water to those dying of thirst, or dough pills to those hypnotised by reports of cures, have little or no positive superiority at all.

To determine the natural status of an Incomplete Monopoly, practically the question we have to ask of it on its positive side is: To what extent has it merit or superiority enough to exclude competition wholly or in part; and to what extent could it absorb all its competitors into a combine or trust? This answered, we have next to turn it over on its reverse or negative side, and ask: To what special risks, other than competition, is it liable in itself?

As regards the first question, we may take English china clay and English steam coal as examples of natural monopolies in their way complete, both from their positive merits and their freedom from foreign competition. Were they in the hands, therefore, of some great Trust, they could take toll from all the world by the prices they could command; but at present they are broken up and divided among a number of separate owners, whose competition among themselves for sales gives away to the buyers a large part of the monopoly selling price which they could so easily command. As for the risks that attend them—there are practically none, either in the mining of the coal or the extraction of the clay, to interfere with the steady amount and regularity of their yield. But not all monopolies are so free from risks as these; and even were they concentrated in single hands, or free from competition among themselves, they are nearly all rendered unstable by unforeseeable risks, which, as we saw with diamonds, must be the case with all high-priced monopoly articles which are not necessaries of life. Special brands of tobacco, wine, or cigars, again, vary in degrees of risk, owing to vicissitudes of climate, weather, atmosphere, soil, insect-pests, and the like; while other monopolies, especially in the case of luxuries, may be made unstable to a disastrous extent by changes in fashion or taste, especially when dealing in commodities where there are possible substitutes; as, for example, in a change from silks to woollens or cottons, from diamonds to emeralds or rubies, from port to sherry or claret or spirits, from Irish whisky to Scotch, from gas to electricity, from horse to motor cabs, electric trams, or omnibuses, and so on.

On the other hand, there are conditions attached to certain Incomplete Monopolies which render them less liable to competition than others. The main condition, perhaps, is the existence of a vast amount of capital at the free disposal of a monopoly in its fight with a rival, especially in those cases where neither can altogether crush out the other by underselling, and yet where to divide the spoil would be to ruin both; as, for example, in the running of two rival railway lines through the same tract of country when there is only business enough for one; or in the sale of commodities the demand for which is limited, and is necessarily confined to a particular area, as in the Professions to a certain extent, and in the great Retail Houses enjoying partial monopolies in separate towns.

Now, in the above and other instances of Incomplete Monopolies, it is evident that even when they are fairly secure on their positive side, the degree of risk varies so much in each case that no definite natural rank can be assigned to them as a class, but only in individual instances after careful investigation of the merits and risks peculiar to each. The most that can be said of them as a class is that they stand in the scale at a point below the rank of stocks founded on Money and on the operation of the Law of Probabilities, like Banks and Insurance Companies, but higher than all other shares in Industrial Businesses making no pretence to monopoly, and, in consequence, controlling neither the buying nor the selling end of their transactions, but subject in both to all the mutations of business and trade.

In the next chapter I propose to deal with those partial monopolies which rest exclusively neither on Money nor on an Industrial basis, but on a combination of both, and are liable to the intrusion of Politics and other extraneous influences as well; and so depend for their natural status on other kinds of security, and are subject to other kinds of risk. But before doing so, we may sum up as far as we have gone by saying that at the summit of the pyramid stand Government stocks as the highest in natural rank, inasmuch as they rest on the broad basis of the entire wealth of the nation itself; and so have an ultimate security above that of all other stocks in the event of a threatening disaster to the State. But it so happens that one of the characteristics of these gilt-edged Government stocks is that they are more sensitive to the intrusion of Political and International Complications than all others;

and are apt, in consequence, to have not only their immediate value, but the supposed stability of their yield, more disturbed than stocks which lie naturally below them in rank; and that, too, over considerable stretches of time, and without any compensation to the investor in a higher yield of interest. In other words, other stocks have often over long periods a degree of practical security as great as that of Government stocks, but with less variation and a greater yield of income. And it is precisely these unnatural inversions of the best Government stocks, often covering considerable periods, through Political or Money Market influences, that give the Geographical Distribution of Capital, as we shall see presently, its golden opportunity. This we shall explain in detail in due course; but in the meantime, returning to our scale of natural values, we may say that immediately below the best Government stocks in natural rank are those stocks which rest primarily on Money and the Law of Probabilities, and are best represented on the large scale by Banks and Insurance Companies. For stability and security they stand as a class as much above any Industrial concerns as in feudal times landed and entailed estates did, with the one exception which we have just seen of Complete Industrial Monopolies which, like the great American Trusts, have secured a control over both the buying and selling ends of the great staple necessaries of life, and which, while as steady and secure as Banks and Insurance Companies, have, by the universal demand for their commodities, a greater yield than they, when confined to a particular country—and *a fortiori* a still greater yield and a still higher status when internationalised.

Below these great Trusts again, as well as below Banks and Insurances, stand the Incomplete Industrial Monopolies which, as we have seen, have control over only one end or limb of their business, but to which as a class no very definite rank can be assigned, inasmuch as each differs from the rest in the extent to which it can defend itself from competition, or can turn itself into a combine, as well as in the special kind and degree of risks to which it is exposed risks, all of them, which render its yield unstable, and its markets capricious and uncertain. And finally, at the bottom of all securities for stability and safety stand the Ordinary shares of ordinary Joint Stock Companies which enjoy no monopoly either in their power of buying or of selling, but are subject to all the accidents and the ups and downs of trade, both in their costs and their yield, and so are beyond the reach of any scientific generalisation. They are the subject-matter, in a word, of speculation and guess-work, so far as the public are concerned; and it is only to those with inside knowledge, as I have already said, that the actual status of any particular one of them can be known. They need not, therefore, concern us here, for my generalisations, rough as they are, must, I repeat, be confined to the different classes of securities, and not to the stock of any particular concern.

CHAPTER III.CORPORATION LOANS, RAILWAY DEBENTURES, ETC.

IN this chapter I propose to consider the natural rank of those securities which are subject to the influence of politics and of Governments, local or central, from which, so far, all private businesses, even the most colossal and complete of monopolies, have been practically free. I shall begin with Corporation Loans, and follow my usual plan of first trying to form some general estimate of their possibilities and outlooks on the positive side as it were, and then, turning them over and looking at them from the reverse or negative side, examine them with the view of determining the nature of the special risks to which they are exposed. To begin with, then, we may say in general that, being Loans, they are founded on Money primarily, and so participate in the relative stability which, as we have seen, attaches to Money values over Industrial ones. In the second place, these Money values, collected from the rates, rest on tangible property, which also has more stability, and over longer periods, than the products of Industry. A third important point about these Corporation Loans is that they are usually sanctioned by the Local Government Board before they are issued; and that, too, after a most careful audit of all the circumstances and conditions, the assets and liabilities, of the municipalities on whose rates they are founded. Besides this, the Government, before sanctioning a Corporation Loan, sees to it that the loan shall be so small in comparison with the rateable property which lies behind it as security, as to be practically beyond the reach of all foreseeable fluctuations or depreciations in the value of that property. Not only so, but the Government takes care also that the term of years which elapses before the loans are redeemable shall be strictly limited to the average length of time during which the works on which the loan is spent are likely to last; and without burdening overmuch future generations of property holders. In buying land, for example, the Government insists that the loan for the purchase of it shall be repaid in from sixty to eighty years; the erection of stone or brick buildings, baths, electric lighting, gasworks, in from twenty to forty years; footways, steamrollers, trees for street improvements and the like, five to ten years, and so on. But even this is not all. The Government is also rigorous in insisting that the rate of interest charged shall be adjusted to the length of the loan—3½ per cent if it does not exceed thirty years, and 3¾ per cent if it does not exceed fifty.

All this is in the interest of and for the protection of the general public who invest in these loans. But the Government looks after the Corporation as well, and prescribes how and when the capital and interest of the loan are to be redeemed: the idea being to make the annual sums as nearly equal as possible throughout the whole period during which the loan has to run. Loans, for example, for periods exceeding thirty years are to be repaid by equal yearly or half-yearly instalments of principal, with interest on the balance of principal from time to time outstanding; while loans for shorter periods are allowed to be paid in equal yearly or half-yearly instalments of principal and interest combined. By means of these and other expedients, the Government has arranged that everything shall be so smoothed and levelled, so square-cut and measured to rule before the loan is floated, that the interest required to meet it shall be kept, as we have seen, at a point of safety so high above all possible or probable fluctuations in the yield from the rates, that these Corporation Loans, while as steady and level in their smaller way as Consols, shall be only just below them in security as well. Indeed, the fact that so many of them in the United Kingdom have been made into Trustee Stocks is only an expression of the public recognition of their high rank as investments. It is true that the loans are expended as often on financially unremunerative as on productive works. Education, bridges, highways, street improvements, sewerage, and parks, for example, yield no pecuniary returns; and as business propositions are apparently nothing but an incubus on the rates. But this is not really so; for it is precisely works of utility, convenience, ornament, or sanitation, like these, that add to the value of the house property on whose rates a large part of the security of these loans is founded; so that they are rather an additional security than a detriment.

If, then, we would sum up the positive merits which the Government in its efforts to protect the public and give it full security has given to these Corporation Loans, we cannot do better, perhaps, than compare them with the comparatively unsheltered and unprotected condition of other stocks. And the first thing that strikes us is, that while other stocks have to depend for their solvency on the limited liability of a limited number of individuals of uncertain means and sources of income, loans to Corporations are secured on the tangible property of whole cities or towns, whose rateable values, besides, can be calculated from year to year almost to a certainty; and so, like an elastic band, can be made to stretch or contract to the yearly requirements of the loan, with the utmost exactitude.

This rateable property, in the second place, has not only an equability of yield and freedom from fluctuation far in excess of any other kind of industrial property, but it has a break-up value far above that of any loan or loans that the Government will allow to be founded on it. Now, this absolute levelness and security of yield, which the elasticity of the rates gives to loans to Corporations, is superior to the general levelness and security of yield which characterise Banks and Insurance Companies from their being founded, as we saw in a previous chapter, on Money and the Law of Probabilities. For the Law of Probabilities, unless, indeed, it can act under such ideal conditions as are present in the Bank of Monte Carlo, can only give you a comparatively rough-hewn levelness and equality of yield, owing to the changes in the Bank rate to which the other Bank rates have to keep time and proportion; while in Insurance Companies the existing tables of chances on which that law has to act are still far from perfect; and so the stability of the yield is imperfect also. But the levelness of the yield of the rates on which the loans to Corporations are founded is guaranteed by the double circumstance, firstly, that if the existing incumbent of a piece of rateable property drops out from death, bankruptcy, or removal, another will usually be found to take his place, the house or building having meanwhile lost little or nothing of its rateable value; and secondly, that if whole regions of streets were deserted in mass, the rest of the Corporation would have to be stretched on the rack until they made good the ensuing deficiency in the rateable yield. Or, to put it differently, we may say that if the fluctuations in the yield of ordinary Industrial and Commercial stock which does not enjoy monopoly may be compared to the troughs and crests of the waves of a gusty sea, and the fluctuations of Banks and Insurance Companies to the ripples on the surface of a calm one, the stability and security of Corporation Loans may be compared to the glassy smoothness of a lake.

But all this, it must be remembered, applies only to Corporation Loans as they leave the hands of the Local Government Board which has sanctioned them; and thus far at least it may be said of them that they do not depend for their continued security on the prudence, honesty, or ability of their managers, as Banks and Insurance Companies partly do, but have in their action the automatic certainty of a machine, which will toss you the yearly proportion of interest and principal into the Stock Redemption Fund and the laps of the stockholders with undeviating precision and directness of aim. From all of which we are forced to conclude that on their positive side at least they have a greater equability and security than either Banks or Insurance Companies, and in consequence a higher natural rank than either. In Great Britain, the best of these loans lie just below the rank of Government stocks, and fully deserve their inclusion among the small exclusive circle of gilt-edged Trustee Securities. But before we can finally sum up their natural status, we must look at their reverse or negative side, and consider the class and degree of risks to which they are liable either now or in the near or more distant future.

Now, these risks, although on the whole slight up to the present, are still definite in character, and make up in the stealthiness of their approach and their potentialities of future growth for their apparent slightness and insignificance. They do not fall suddenly, like the earthquakes or devastating fires to which Insurance Companies are occasionally liable; nor do they come with the unexpectedness of Bank panics; but are so slow and insidious in their approach and operation that were it not for the publicity of the Press, to which the affairs of the Corporations lie open, the initial care and discretion exercised by the Local Government Board before it sanctions these loans would afford but a very imperfect protection against the accidents and risks to which they are liable before they have run their full course. Still, even in this respect their risks are less than those of Banks, which in times of crisis or panic have no defence whatever against calamity, even when they escape ruination. The ordinary reserves of Banks are not in themselves sufficient to be of any avail, and the class of collateral securities to which they are legitimately confined, namely, those which can command instant sale, or convertibility into cash at a moment's notice without loss, are not of a kind which they can afford to hold in sufficient quantity over a long enough period of time to meet these crises. And when once their reserves are exhausted they have nothing of importance but their unpaid-up capital to fall back upon; and this can neither be got together quickly enough, nor, if it could, would the call for it in most cases spell anything but ruin to many of the shareholders.

But, on the other hand, there are a number of risks to which Corporation Loans are liable, from which both Banks and Insurance Companies are altogether free; and these it is necessary to distribute into their respective categories before the net amount of risk attaching to them can be appraised and summed up for the investor's consideration.

The first and most obvious risk in Corporation Loans is the danger that the money may be spent in hare-brained, unproductive enterprises which bring in either no return at all, or only after many years, during which time the interest and Redemption Fund have to be punctually paid. This, however, is a risk to which I attach comparatively little importance, especially in this country, where the loan has to run the gauntlet of the inspection and sanction of the Local Government Board before it can be floated. It is only of importance in the case of the Corporation Loans of foreign countries, where neither the Government inspection and sanction can be relied on to prevent disaster, nor yet can the details and circumstances of the Corporation be sufficiently known to outsiders to make the security other than problematical guesswork. On the other hand, many of these foreign Corporation Loans may all the time have all the security of the best English stocks, and with a higher rate of interest as well; and it is here that, as we shall see later on, the Geographical Distribution of Capital comes to the help of the investor.

The real risks proceed from quite another quarter, and are not only much more incalculable but much more insidious in their operation. The first is a purely speculative and, to a large extent, unforeseeable risk; the second inheres in the very nature of these loans, and it is to be feared will become more and more dangerous in the future. The first may be summed up in the danger of the leading trades and industries of the towns or cities which have contracted these loans (and with them the population dependent on them), stealing away more slowly or rapidly to new and more favoured regions for the exercise of their callings; especially when the town or city depends for its general prosperity on the continued prosperity of some special industry for which it has acquired a reputation. This might easily arise, for example, if a tariff which had protected a particular industry from the inroads of foreign competition were suddenly withdrawn—as in the case of Spitalfields with its silk industry and other well-known instances. But a still more dangerous, because more permanent and irremediable, risk would arise if the population of the town or city declined, not merely, as sometimes occurs, through changes in fashion, as in watering-places and the like, but through its trade being stolen away by the discovery of a centre *in the same country* more favourable for its exercise.

Now, in old historic nations this is altogether unlikely, inasmuch as the evolution which has fixed the present great industries in the localities they now occupy is the result of a process of selection and weeding-out of the less favoured regions, continued through generations and centuries. Either the raw materials of the industry exist in the neighbourhood in the most accessible form and the greatest abundance, as in the case of the steel and iron works in the Midlands and the North of England; or the particular trade centre owes its success to the cheap and easy transmission of its products to the outside world by railway, canal, river, or sea, as in ship-building centres on the Clyde, at Belfast, and elsewhere; or in virtue of its possessing the peculiar qualities of soil, air, or climate necessary to the highest development of the commodities—as the moisture of the air in the centres of the cotton industry, the quality of the water in the great brewing centres, or what not.

In all these instances it is quite improbable that the local conditions on which towns or cities depend for the growth of their population, and for the continuance of their manufacturing or commercial prosperity, should ever again be affected by the discovery of more favoured spots in these old countries; or that their rateable values in consequence should ever fall below the liabilities which these towns and cities have contracted for the repayment of their loans.

Now, this would not necessarily be so in young countries, still sparsely populated and with hidden resources of all kinds still awaiting development, and where, in consequence, the great future trading centres only twinkle dimly here and there in the twilight. This is especially true in the case of mines as yet unknown. As in the past so in the future of these young and still undeveloped countries; gold mines like those of California, Australia, South Africa, and Klondike; silver mines like those of Nevada; diamond mines as in South Africa; coal and iron as in Canada; oil wells as in Russia or the East, may be suddenly discovered in the most unlikely regions; with the result that, in their immediate neighbourhood, great trading centres and populations, thus artificially created, may arise like gourds in a night, but on the exhaustion of the mines as suddenly wither and disappear—and with them the rateable values on which their Corporation Loans were raised. All this is, of course, true but trite, and needs but little further labouring here.

But in the present state of the world there are other risks of a more serious and insidious kind, which, although at present neither imminent nor pressing, are not at all unlikely to become increasingly so in the near or more distant future. For in these Corporation Loans we touch on the first intrusion of Local Politics into industrial and business concerns. They lie on those outlying points on the circumference where the worlds of politics and business intersect; and where the virus or virtues of the one can readily interpenetrate the other; at those points, namely, where the Local self-government of cities and municipalities is the most remote and free from control by the Central Power. It may well be worth our while, therefore, to glance at them for a moment in this connection, with a view of defining more carefully the class of

Governments that are the most liable to, or most exempt from, this intrusion.

In most of the old Oriental countries, private businesses have little or no immunity from the incursions either of the Central or the Local Powers; as we have seen in countries like Turkey, Egypt, Persia, and India (before the British occupation), where these incursions were the standing curse for ages and worked to the ruin of wealth, credit, and industry alike. Nor, again, in young countries, where neither the security of person nor property has had time to become inviolate through the hardening and consolidating forces of custom and tradition, is there as yet a full immunity from the incursions either of the Central or the Local Powers. It is different in all the old European countries, where law and order, and especially the sacredness of private property, are most jealously safeguarded; for there the security of individual businesses from the intrusions of politicians into their management has up to the present been the last sacred ark to be touched either by the political commotions of the country, by international complications, or by war itself. But it is not in old *centralised* Administrations like that of France, for example, that danger lies. The dangers to Corporation Loans from the political side are, curiously enough, to be apprehended in old democratic Governments like those of America and England, where local self-government and laissez-faire have been carried to their most extreme points. For in these countries it is possible—by reason of this very sacredness of local self-government—for Borough Councils or Boards of Guardians to make a raid on the rates through the back door as it were, and to "sweat" them for unproductive purposes, even when they are safeguarded at the front door, as we have seen, by the Central Government whose permission is necessary before most of these Corporation Loans can be issued.

Take America, for example, where local self-government is so rigorously safeguarded by the Constitution, and what do we see? Local political "Bosses" exploiting the rates for the benefit of themselves or their political and business friends to a degree almost unexampled in any other civilised country. Now, these Bosses and Magnates are intense individualists, and so are the American people themselves as yet; but how would it fare with the rates, and with the Corporation Loans secured on them, if, instead of Bosses and their henchmen, their Municipal Councils were packed with Socialists who, on their own avowed principles, are determined by inroads into Capital to support great masses of the population out of the rates? The process has already begun in England, where, as we have seen in the case of West Ham, whole sections of the population have been maintained through this back-door sweating of individual businesses through the rates, with but little power of direct interference by the Central Government after once a loan is floated; and with the result that old-established businesses employing many workmen are obliged to leave these localities and to carry their establishments elsewhere, to the greater or less detriment of the rates on which the Corporation Loans are secured.

Now, if these things are getting a foothold here, what security can there be for the future of Corporation Loans anywhere? And especially in the younger democracies where the security of private property as such has not yet become a sacred tradition. It is true that the leakage of the rates from the intrusion of Socialists into Borough Councils and Boards of Guardians is at present a negligible quantity; but West Ham is a warning that under local Socialist Administration neither the growth of population nor the rateable value of property would be sufficient to secure adequately against depreciation the existing Corporation Loans, even when the Central Government itself was altogether free from any Socialistic taint. To sum up, then, I take it that in spite of the careful inspection and supervision of these loans by the existing Government before they are issued, in spite of the elasticity of the rates which secure them under legal compulsion, as well as of the remoteness of the chance of Central Governments themselves becoming purely Socialistic in character; in spite of all this, these Corporation Loans are not as safe, so far as their future outlook is concerned, as the majority of investors in them imagine them to be. Aggressive Socialism, however much it may profess to attain its end by striking directly at the Central Government, can have no chance of success until it has previously secured majorities in its favour in the local Borough Councils, Boards of Guardians, and Parliamentary Selection Committees—as, indeed, Mr. Sidney Webb and Mr. Bernard Shaw have, by the propaganda which they carried on for years by way of these back doors, clearly shown. But as Socialism is a growing force in all civilised countries at the present time, and therefore must permeate more and more the composition of these local Councils of all kinds as time goes on, it may be safely predicted that unless Local Government officials, in democratic States at least, are more directly controlled by the Central Power than they are to-day, never again will Corporation Loans possess that high rank for stability and security which they enjoyed in the past, unless, indeed, by direct Government or National guarantee.

And now a word or two on the security and risks of those stocks which, like Corporation Loans, rest primarily on a Money basis, and this in turn on a definite Industrial one—unlike Banks and Insurances, which rest on that basis more remotely and indefinitely—and which contain, besides, elements of Monopoly, partial or complete. Among such stocks the Debentures of Railway Companies take a high natural rank. To begin with, these companies usually enjoy either a full or partial monopoly of traffic to and from the great business centres, whose industries they unite and whose products they transport to the remotest ramifications of their system. Unless, therefore, these great industrial centres themselves decay, the Railway Debentures ought, when sufficiently secured against the ups and downs of trade, to form one of the safest of securities. This will apply even to small lines with little capital at their back, provided always they are the necessary connecting links between other great lines, and so have even a greater monopoly value than either of the separate lines which they connect.

In young countries with great potential but as yet undeveloped wealth, these Railway Debentures have a high potential natural value even where their income does not as yet yield a dividend on their Ordinary shares—from the mere fact of the large measure of monopoly which, when the country is fully developed, they are almost sure to enjoy over large fields and areas of production. To fix their natural value as securities, then, it is the risks that must mainly be kept in mind. As to these, we may say in general terms that they avoid the great standing risks to which Banks and Insurance Companies are exposed in the shape of crises, panics, earthquakes, and vast destructive fires, while being liable to all those risks which must necessarily inhere in loans based on the ups and downs of Trade and Industry, as distinct from those which, like Banks and Insurances, rest primarily on Money and the level operation over most of their field of the Law of Probabilities.

As Monopolies, or partial Monopolies, they are not as free from risk as those purely Industrial Monopolies which deal in the great necessities of life Oil, Beef, Soap, Sugar, and the like—inasmuch as these can not only fix their selling prices on an even level above their costs, but can coerce, to a great extent, and secure their customers as well—except when the public can slip the noose by the use of some substitute, as they have been doing in America with the Beef Trust; whereas the yield of the Railways on which the Debentures are issued, not only varies according to the state of trade, but the trades on which it depends do not necessarily rest on the supply of articles either of necessity or universal demand. And the consequence is that while the great Industrial Trusts can nearly always hit the mark both of price and profit which they set before themselves, the Railway Companies have to take chances of hitting their target amidst the hills and valleys and the ups and downs of Trade.

Again, these Railway Debentures being loans—and, therefore, resting primarily on Money—have less security, while subject to the same kind of risk as Corporation Loans. For while the Corporation Loans are secured on the property of a whole community, and on rates which not only have all the elasticity required for that security, but are enforced by law with the utmost rigour, Railway Debentures are secured only on the property of their own particular shareholders, and on the wide and deep fluctuations of good and bad trade. They differ, therefore, as much from Corporation Loans in the safety of their securities as the old unlimited liability Banks of years gone by—which made shareholders liable to the full extent of their fortune—do from the Limited Liability Banks of to-day, which make them liable only to the limited amount of their investment. Nor is this lesser security on the part of Railway Debentures made up by the absence of any risk to which Corporation Loans either now or in the future are likely to be exposed. For they, too, like Corporation Loans, lie on the border-line where politics and business intersect and commingle, and so can be "sweated" through the rates by local politicians with Socialistic proclivities in the same way, if not to the same extent, as they. On the whole, then, summing up the pros and cons, I should be inclined to say that for investment purposes over equal periods of time, Corporation Loans have less fluctuation, and so occupy, perhaps, a higher natural rank than Railway Debentures; and *a fortiori* than all other Industrial Debentures which do not enjoy, like Railway Companies, a full or partial Monopoly.

And this brings us to those Debentures which rest on partial or complete Monopolies, in the sense, that is to say, that they have certain privileges accorded to them by Municipal or other authorities exempting them from competition over the whole or a part of their field of operations. Among these stocks may be mentioned those of Waterworks, Gas or Electric Lighting, Tramways, and the like; and what we have now to do is to ascertain the general principles which determine their natural rank in the scale of securities. These may be ranged under the following heads:

1. The amount of natural Monopoly they contain in themselves, as it were.

2. The extent to which they can be kept free from competition. It will be remembered, perhaps, that in a former chapter I defined a complete Industrial Monopoly as one which could control not only its buying end, but its selling end, besides making level the intervening distance as well. It may be remembered, also, that in order to get some ideal standard of comparison for the ranking of those stocks which, like Banks and Insurance Companies, rest primarily on Money, I selected the Bank of Monte Carlo as my ideal of comparison.

We now have to find some parallel ideal for stocks which, like these Water, Gas, Electricity, Trams, and others, rest on an Industrial basis, and possess a quasi-Monopoly in their own sphere. And the ideal I would suggest would be that of a stock which in a forecast would have a predicability along its whole course; or, to put it differently, of a stock which could be taken out of private hands to-morrow and with a little stoking and oiling could be nationalised or municipalised, and when once set going would run of itself on a track made smooth and level for it from beginning to end. Now, the characteristics which an ideal stock of this kind, resting on an Industrial basis, should have, may be summed up in the following particulars, namely: that when the cost price of the materials used in its processes is known, the sale price should be fixable, the customers averageable, the reserve needed for repairs calculable, that its freedom from competition should be assured, that there should be no available substitutes for it, no "goodwill" or "water" in its composition, and no chance of political or other outside intrusions making or marring its fortunes.

Now, these are the constituents of any ideal stock which is based on Industry and enjoys a Monopoly in its own line. Indeed, for stocks resting on an industrial basis, these conditions are as ideal as those which, on a Money basis, hedge round the Bank of Monte Carlo itself; and precisely in so far as any stock falls short in any of these particulars in any forecast of its future fortunes, so far will its rank be lower for investment purposes in the scale both of stability and security. In other words, given an Industrial Monopoly, complete or partial, the degree of ease, accuracy, and precision with which forecasts of its returns can be made, is a measure of the stability of the stock for investment purposes; whereas the opposite will be the measure of its instability and insecurity, inasmuch as all will then depend on the business acumen and penetration of its managers—an asset which is as uncertain in its tenure as their individual lives.

If we apply these principles, then, to Water, Gas, Electricity, Trams, and other companies which enjoy complete Monopolies as against other companies of the same kind, but which are subject to the competition of companies supplying alternative products, it will be obvious that a Water Debenture Stock ought to hold almost ideal natural rank in point of security—a higher rank than Railway Debentures, as being freer from the ups and downs of trade on which the railways depend; higher than Corporation Loans, as avoiding the danger of Capital being expended on unproductive undertakings or squandered by "Bosses" and intruding politicians; higher than all but the closest of those Monopolies which deal in the other necessities of life, inasmuch as there is no alternative product that can at all supply its place; higher than Gas or Electric Stocks, which are alternatives to, or substitutes for, one another, and are still engaged in a fighting competition among themselves for supremacy, and so split the market in a way that makes a forecast of their customers difficult, if not impossible; higher than Trams, Motors, and Omnibuses, which are also in their transitional fighting stage, and at best have not quite the same necessity attached to their use, and so cannot be assured of any definite division of the spoils.

And now a word or two on those ordinary Industrial Debentures which have neither Monopoly, Charter, nor Guarantee at their back. Of these the natural rank is determined in quite a different way; namely, by the amount and quality of the Capital that lies at the back of the Debentures as their security. Indeed it may be said that they have no natural rank, but may lie anywhere in the gamut from the most gilt-edged of securities down to the fluctuating level of ordinary business shares. All will depend on the amount of tangible, realisable, industrial plant which, in the event of a break-up sale, lies behind them in each individual case.

If, for example, the Capital at the back of these Debentures is sunk in tangible property, freehold or leasehold, land, buildings, or plant, with a relatively high break-up value on a forced sale, it is well; but if half of it, say, is made up of mere goodwill, or patent rights almost time-expired, or depends on the lives of managers of exceptional ability, it is not so well. But if the security of the Debentures rests almost entirely on goodwill, without a Monopoly property site of exceptional attractions to back it, or on businesses which have been paying exceptionally high dividends without exceptional qualifications whereby to limit or prevent competition, it must, in the swift, changing fluctuations of the modern industrial world, be not well at all. Mr. Lowenfeld, in his book (*All About Investment*), has admirably summed up the whole matter in a passage which runs to the following effect: "If Money is invested in the Debentures of such concerns as can show twice as much of their Capital in Preference and Ordinary shares as they have in their Debentures; in concerns which have, further, a ten or fifteen years' history of solid business with a narrow range of fluctuation; and, again, can show profits which will cover the interest of these Debentures at least three times over, and, besides, always keep a good deal more of cash or liquid assets on hand than will meet their current liabilities—then you may consider them as safe over a very considerable length of time as even the most gilt-edged of securities. For it would indeed go hard with them if, thus amply secured, the break-up value of their assets would not be sufficient to redeem the capital of these Debentures at their original price." Besides, as we shall see later, such Debentures are less subject to the intrusions of the political complications of the outside world, or the intrusions of home and local politics, than Government Securities themselves.

As for the Ordinary shares of ordinary Joint Stock Companies, depending as they do on the ups and downs of commerce and industry at every point in their course, they may be said to be beyond the range of definite forecast either on their cost side or their selling side, either in the ordinary competition or in the new-inventions and processes which they may have to encounter, and so are and must be the subject-matter of speculation rather than of investment for stability and security, and need not concern us further here. Like pariahs, they have no inherent natural rank, but at best have to be taken on trust by all except those who have inside knowledge of their particular character and working. They are, indeed, the standing danger of the investing world, owing to the facility with which they lend themselves to fraud and delusion; and the only protection the public has against them lies in the knowledge of how to read their balance-sheets with penetration and discretion. The law itself has in recent years given the shareholders and the public every facility for forcing a full disclosure of the affairs of all these Limited Joint Stock Companies, whenever their audited balance-sheets are either too abstruse or obscure for adequate comprehension. But the shareholders rarely insist on this, and prefer rather to trust to the reports of their Boards of Directors, under the illusion that the interest of the directors and the shareholders must necessarily be one. It would be both interesting and appropriate at this point to retail some of the methods by which the books of a company are falsified by swindling directors, but as my space is limited I shall be obliged to defer this until some future occasion.

And now, having attempted to determine, in a rough kind of way, the relative natural rank of the various orders of stocks and securities, I shall proceed in the succeeding chapters to deal with a still more important aspect of our problem, and one, too, to which all we have as yet said leads up—namely, those principles, both of Money Markets and of Industrial Exchanges, which cause an inversion of this natural rank among securities, and so make a Geographical Distribution of Capital among the various nations and divisions of the world a source at once of greater revenue, greater stability, and greater security than the most gilt-edged stocks of any single nation.

CHAPTER IV.THE EFFECT OF POLITICS, STOCK EXCHANGES AND MONEY MARKETS

IN our previous chapters we endeavoured to get some rough general idea of what may be called the natural ranking of the various classes of stocks in point at once of security, stability, and freedom from fluctuation. But before this knowledge can be of much value for purposes of investment, it is necessary not only to know the natural value and rank of these different classes of securities, but also to ascertain in any given case whether it is possible for outside causes to have intervened to throw one or more of them out of their natural order; and if so, where we are to look for the causes which give rise to such displacements; just as in prospecting for coal it is necessary not only to know the natural lie of the coal seams in the series of geological strata, but to ascertain whether from upheaval or subsidence this natural order of superposition has been artificially inverted, and lower rocks have been thrown on the top of those naturally higher in the scale—to the confusion of the unwary prospector.

Now, it is well known on every Stock Exchange that whole classes of securities are continually changing their natural ranking in one or other part of the world, owing to the intrusion of outside influences of one kind or another. Our problem, then, in this chapter is to try and ascertain what these perverting and thwarting influences are, and how they operate in changing and inverting the relative values of different securities, often over considerable periods of time.

In a general way I may say, to begin with, that the key to the whole situation lies in the influence exercised over the values of all other stocks in any given country by the rate of interest of the Government Stocks of that country; and, secondly, in the relative state of the Money Markets of the different countries. For the general effect of these Money

Market influences is this, that Government Stocks, which naturally lie at the very top of the pyramid of securities, decline to a point lower in the scale than stocks naturally much inferior to them in status; and so give the prudent investor an opportunity to select for investment stocks which will give him not only a greater yield of interest, but an equal, if not higher, level of stability than the Government Stocks themselves. For it must be remembered that one of the peculiarities of Government Stocks, which separates them off from all other stocks, is that, being secured on all the industries of a nation alike, and having a first mortgage on them all, as it were, they cannot rise in value from any cause without pulling all other stocks up in market value with them, or fall in value without dragging all the rest down; and this, too, without the real *industrial* value of these other stocks having been in any way altered. And the consequence of this again is, that if the investor can only ascertain which of the Government Stocks of the world happen to be behaving in this abnormal way, he can, with the exercise of a little vigilance, be almost sure of getting a larger yield of income, and with less fluctuation in the yield, than if he invested entirely in the most gilt-edged of Government securities. But this involves that the investor should have at his disposal the stocks of the world from which to make a selection, and not those of any single nation alone. If, for example, he were investing his money in English Government or Trustee Stocks exclusively, he would be liable to find that during the ordinary term which a stock held for investment purposes (and not for speculation) has to run, its value might decline very appreciably from the price at which it was bought, as has been seen in the case of Consols during the last twenty years. It is true that it might rise as well as fall; but that would be as much a case of speculation among stocks of high lineage as ordinary Stock Exchange speculation is among the Ordinary shares of stocks of lower rank. In such a case, indeed, the simple and unsuspecting investor who went on the idea that Government Stocks were not only the safest but the most stable of securities, because they had at their back the entire resources of the State, and so could borrow at the lowest rate of interest, would find himself very much disappointed. But our problem here is how to eliminate speculation and risk, and to give to our investment list something of the stability and security of the stocks which rest on Money and the application of the Law of Probabilities. I do not mean to say that there are not other causes besides the price of Government Stocks which give rise to a variation in the market value of other Loan Stocks, when no change has occurred in the real intrinsic value of the stocks themselves. Far from it, as we shall presently see; but the tidal influence of Government Stocks in drawing all other Loan Stocks after them is, like that of the moon, a real and absolute one, although counteracted or helped by other influences as well. I have mentioned it here, in passing, in order that the reader may see that, if this be true, the investor who wishes to get the greatest yield for his money with a minimum of instability, and with the greatest practical security for the return of his capital unimpaired, must stretch his view beyond the limits of his own country and be prepared to embrace some scheme of Geographical Distribution among the different nations of the world—if it can be found. But what difference would a geographical distribution make if all Loan Stocks follow the Government Stocks of their respective countries? the reader may ask. What better security would there be in them all than in any one in particular?

To begin with, there would be much, if it should be found that the different Government Stocks of the world could be arranged like flowers in a circlet, where some stood erect at the top of the stem, each with its own country's other stocks ranged below it in natural rank and gradation, and others again so drooped that they lay lower down in the hierarchy than stocks which, like the best Corporation Loans or Industrial Debentures, naturally lie below them in the scale. If this fact can be established, would it not be possible for a wary investor to pick out the best secured of these Debentures and Corporation Stocks in the particular countries where the Government Stocks had lost their position at the head of the list, and so get not only as much practical security, but a greater yield of interest and a less width of fluctuation than if he had invested entirely in Government Stocks? I believe it would be possible, for several reasons.

In the first place, the interest would be higher, because in every country the rate of interest from all other stocks is always fixed higher than the rate of interest on the Government Stocks.

In the second place, the stability of the other stocks would be greater and their range of fluctuations less than that of the Government Stocks, inasmuch as most of the political and other causes which depress the value of Government Stocks affect the best secured Industrial Loans, as we shall see, comparatively slightly.

In the third place, by taking the whole world as our field of investment, the different Money Market influences and Trade currents of the particular nations can be balanced against each other under categories so definite as to permit of the principle of Insurance being applied to them; and with a degree of certainty, too, not to be found in the stocks of any one country, which, under the same Money Market and Trade influences, necessarily all move up and down together.

With these preliminaries the reader will have some vague general idea of what it is I wish to prove; and I shall now ask him to accompany me while I attempt to make good in detail the several positions I have raised. The evidence I have collected comes from various quarters of the financial field; but as it is made up of a mixture of facts and principles, I shall be obliged to take them separately, with the understanding that it is only when we have got them all together that the part played by any one of them in the final conclusion which I shall attempt to draw, can be clearly seen.

I shall begin with the first paradox of which I imagine the reader will wish to see a definite explanation given—the paradox, namely, of why it is that Government Stocks, which stand naturally at the head of all other stocks in point of security (as shown by the low rate of interest which they yield the investor in them), should be subject to fluctuations in market value more violent than those of stocks much lower in the scale? The reasons are various, but the most general one is that, in the first place, the stability of Government Stocks is based primarily on *political* causes, that of all other stocks on *industrial* ones. Not that both causes, as we have seen in a former chapter, do not enter more or less into all securities, but rather that Government Stocks lie more open to, and are also more sensitive to, political influences than all other stocks whatever. They lie more open to them, because they occupy, as in battle, the firing line; for as a result of a war to-morrow, in which a whole nation might change its masters, while private business might remain untouched except in a *pro rata* increase of taxation, Government Stocks would be struck to the heart through the depressing effects of vague financial fear alone.

A private Industrial Debenture Stock in an old-standing business which has, say, twice as much Ordinary capital at the back of its Debenture loan as the amount of the loan itself, and which has earned, say, three times as much dividend over a period of ten to fifteen years as is necessary to pay the interest on the loan, is generally regarded as a thoroughly reliable stock for investment purposes, both in point of security and stability. But a Government Stock, on the other hand, that was based on a national income of the same amount, i.e. of not more than three times the yield of its taxes, would fall from its high estate and sink to a point as low as that of Turkey in the olden days. But why this difference between the amount of security required to give a first-class gilt-edged character to a private stock and that required for a

Government Stock? Clearly there must be some elements or factors concerned, apart from Industry and its products and values.

What, then, are they? To begin with, it is evident that as Government Stocks do not vary mainly with the ups and downs of business as all other stocks do, they must vary with what must fall under the head of Political complications in one shape or another. But this can only be because in some way the financial security of the National Stock is affected by the political complications; for investors will not lose their sleep over political complications that are not likely to touch their pockets. And, indeed, when we look closely, we see that there are several ways, short of the expropriation of territory, in which political troubles may affect a nation's financial security and stability.

In the first place, we have the somewhat far-fetched, but nevertheless real, moral, and psychological fact, viz., that the Public Conscience, which is ultimately responsible for a Government Loan, is not as reliable an asset as is the private conscience of a private firm in the discharge of private business debts, as the income tax returns would show; nor, what is more important, is there any law enforceable against a nation that refuses to pay its public debts, as there is in the case of private firms.

In the second place, in most civilised countries, even those of uncertain political stability, national debts are spread fairly equally over all classes of the people; and to them all classes contribute either through direct or indirect taxation. But it is to be observed that it is only the Property-holders and the Employers of Labour on whom in a national emergency the Government could rely to make good any such large increase of taxation as would be involved in a great and unsuccessful war; the rest of the population being, like the proverbial Highlander, without anything on which an additional levy can be made with assurance of success; as would be seen, for example, if it were attempted to throw the increased taxation of a large and unsuccessful war on the rent or salt-tax of the Hindu taxpayers, swarming in their millions though they be.

The Capitalist Classes stand in the fighting line, as we have said, and are the first to bear the brunt of taxation caused by Political complications. And although in the end the increased tax is usually fairly enough distributed among all classes of the population, still the fewness in number of the employing and property-holding classes, and the magnitude of the financial risks they run in proportion to their numbers in the event of an adverse issue, so affect the imagination, that they throw the Government Stocks into a state of commotion and fluctuation more violent than that of any other stocks whatever. For most businesses, ministering as they do to the necessaries and conveniences of everyday life, would go on more or less as usual in face of any but the most imminent and pressing political complications; and the capitalists and property-holders are quite well aware of the fact.

And when we remember that it is these capitalists and property-holders almost exclusively who regulate the Money Market; and, further, that it is the Money Market, with Government Stocks at the top, that regulates the price of all the stocks below them in the scale which, like Debentures and Corporation Stocks, are founded on Money; when we remember that this rise or fall is quite independent of any change in the *industrial* or business bases of these stocks—the loans all falling in value with the fall of Government Stocks and rising with their rise—when we remember all this, we can see how it is that Government Stocks, which always stand in point of ultimate security at the head of all other stocks in a nation, may not only have a less yield of interest, but a greater fluctuation and less value over periods of time sufficiently long for investment purposes, than stocks like Corporation Loans and Industrial Debentures, naturally much lower in the scale of securities. In a word, the best stocks of a country, the Government Stocks, while always paying less interest than other stocks, are often less stable for purposes of investment as well.

But there are other reasons equally important for the more violent fluctuations of Government Stocks over other Loans, not only in times of political uncertainty but of industrial or business uncertainty; and these may all be summed up in the conditions of the Money Market, strictly so called, which permanently mark off Government Stocks from all others.

The first is the relation between the state of the Money Market and the state of Trade. If trade is brisk and industrial operations expanding, capital is withdrawn from Government Stocks and invested in Industrial operations for the sake of their greater yield; and Government Stocks in consequence remain depressed. On the other hand, if credit is slack and trade depressed from any cause, Government Stocks become a haven of refuge until the danger passes by, and so far rise; but it is the passage upwards of a sick and wounded, not a healthy, activity.

Again, if the Money Market is depleted from any cause—new Loans to Government, Foreign Loans, etc.—Government Stocks still remain depressed from the difficulty of finding customers at their low rate of interest, and from the temptation to the investor to rush into mere Stock Exchange speculation in consequence. It is true they are always in request as collateral for Bank advances, and as taking the place of cash itself at a sufficient discount; but as they enter at one door they quickly pass out by the other; and so in jog-trot times the purchases and sales of Government Stocks pretty well balance each other, and their market quotations still remain practically where they were.

It is the same, too, with the large demand that always exists for Government Stocks as Trustee investments, as well as for their use as collateral to meet the lighter temporary exigencies of the Government itself; so that, in ordinary times, and for all *temporary* fluctuations of business credit, Government Stocks swing lazily backwards and forwards in a state of moving equilibrium, with even less demand when trade is brisk, credit good, and money plentiful, than when trade is depressed, credit shaky, and money scarce. The only *permanent* condition which can cause a steady rise in the value of Government Stocks is such an increase of the real *productive* wealth of a country as will give it both the increased power of paying its debts and the increased willingness to do so—a state of things which registers itself on the financial barometer by a fall in the rate of interest, and a lessened yield of income to investors.

On the other hand, as a set-off against this necessarily slow rise of Government Stocks in the best of times, we have the sudden precipitation with which they plunge down in times of International trouble, Political crises, or Internal revolution; or in times of great and sudden withdrawals of money from the Money Market for loans to which the ordinary requirements of business continuity and development have not had time to adapt themselves.

So that, summing up these various considerations as a whole, it would appear that in Government Stocks we have a species of security which, affected as it is so much more by Political events than other stocks, has a tendency always to run down on the slightest provocation, but to rise slowly and tentatively only on the most potent and real demonstrations of increased national wealth. From all of which it is evident that, however superior in ultimate security Government stocks may be over all other stocks in the same country, they are not practically as sound for investment purposes as the best Corporation Loans or Industrial Debentures, when regard is had at once to the lower yield of interest of Government Stocks, to their greater range of fluctuation, and to their greater tendency to fall on the least provocation rather than rise on the strongest inducement.

Then there is the fact that while other loans have their range of fluctuation determined mainly by general Money Market influences, the speculations in them on the Stock Exchange, as well as by the prosperity of the Industries on which they rest, Government Stocks vary not only with all these influences, but with the state of the Political sky as well; and so their range of fluctuation is greater. And as they do not rise like other stocks in periods when Trade is booming, but only after long periods during which the permanent wealth of the country has steadily increased, their unnatural depressions are not only deeper but more abiding. And when we have added to this again the fact that the best of the other stocks have in Britain now been made Trustee Stocks, we can have but little hope that English Consols, at least, will rise appreciably for a long time.

But there are other countries that have Government Stocks besides Great Britain, and before we can see the way in which a Geographical Distribution of Capital among these other nations can advantage the investor, we must ascertain what relation these Foreign Government Stocks bear to our own Consols and to each other, as well as to the other stocks of their respective countries.

To begin with, then, we may say that just as there is a hierarchy in the natural rank of the various stocks of the same country, so, too, is there a hierarchy among the Government Stocks of different countries, Great Britain standing at the head of the list, and being able to borrow at the present time at a 3 per cent interest; while the United States, France, and Germany have to pay somewhere nearer 4 per cent; Italy and Austria still more; Japan and Russia over 5 per cent, and so on; and to this we may add that in each of these countries all other bonds whatever take their cue and point of departure in the rate of interest they will be expected to pay, from the Government Stock of that particular country, having to pay more and more interest as they descend the scale; and, further, that each nation in the main considers that its own Government Securities are the best.

Now, it may be freely admitted that it is not likely that the above rates of interest will be found to do more than approximately represent the real relative security in the future of these Foreign Government Stocks in their relation to each other; but this we may affirm with certainty, that they are as near the existing truth as human calculation and foresight can make them. For, like the relative positions and distances of the stars, they have been fixed by the great world-financers who, like astronomers with their telescopes, are stationed at different points on the axle of the great revolving wheel of World Industry and Finance; and, as nation after nation passes successively before them, fix the meridian points, as it were, of the financial stability and security of each, before passing them over to the public and the Stock Exchange for Money Market and other influences to work their will on them in their future rise or fall.

It is these world-financers who float, underwrite, or otherwise by their influence finance the loans of Foreign Governments; they bear the full brunt and risk of the loans in the first instance; and as they may at any moment be called upon to send in estimates for them, it is their business to know all that can be practically known of the financial status and of the industrial resources of foreign countries, as well as what may be legitimately hazarded by way of prediction in the matter of their future prospects. They can speak with authority on the *past* financial history of these countries, their previous loans, and on what they have been spent—whether on *productive* labour on the one hand, and the opening up of new sources of industry which will add to the country's wealth; or in military expenses and armaments, in corruption, in the payment of old debts, or in fruitless internal revolutions or foreign wars, on the other. And when in relation to all this they have taken into consideration the *existing industrial* resources of the country in question, and its power of development in the near or immediate future, they are then able to compare these total resources and drawbacks with the weight of taxation which the country is able to bear, either at the present time or later; and as the result of it all to fix what may be called the *natural* rate of interest on a loan to that particular country.

But before we can see clearly how it is that capital may be distributed and invested among these foreign countries with a greater scientific certainty and security and stability than in the home investments of any particular country, it is necessary that we should resolve this natural rate of interest of these Government Loans into its component parts, with the view of exhibiting the part played in it by each of these parts respectively. The first part consists of what may be termed the Political factor; the second of the Money Market factor; and the third of the Industrial factor. Of these the Political factor is the most uncertain and the least scientific in character, but, like a dangerous object seen through a haze, it has, through its influence on the imagination, and the anxiety to ensure a sufficient margin of safety under any contingency, a greater effect in raising the rate of interest to be paid on Government Loans (and, in consequence, in raising the rate that has to be paid on every Corporation Loan, Railway Debenture, or Joint Stock Industrial Debenture in the country, however well-secured, industrially speaking, these latter may be) than it ought legitimately to have.

Should there be any elements of political danger or instability in the form of Government of the country; any elements of corruption in its habitual administration; any danger of insurrection; any tendency to plunder the capitalist classes by exorbitant or capricious taxation, by badly laid tariffs or the absence of tariffs, or by direct taxation laid on the instruments of production; any tampering with the currency; any danger of war with neighbouring Powers, and the like—should any, or most, of these conditions be present in a country, it is only natural that the rate of interest it has to pay for loans should rise to a point higher than it ought to be, or than it would be were there any possibility of treating these separate loans to Foreign Powers by a distribution of the risks among them as in an insurance company; or as would be the case, most probably, if there were only a single great financial house in the world which had the exclusive patronage of them all.

But although Governments have to pay for their vagaries by having the rate of interest raised on their loans, there is no reason why private businesses or Joint Stock Industrial Companies should have their rates of interest also raised in proportion, provided they are sufficiently secured otherwise; for, as we saw in a former chapter, private business concerns dealing with the manufacture, transportation, or sale of the staple and customary necessaries and luxuries of life, are comparatively safe in times of political disturbance, and would hardly be more depreciated in value by a revolution than Government Stocks, in times of threatened insurrection, would be by a street riot.

Now, the part played by this Political factor in the composition of the rate of interest of a Government Loan, great as it is, is usually absorbed and embodied in the second factor, viz., that of the Money Market which reflects it, but which has, besides, a distinct status and individuality of its own apart from the influence of Politics and political movements as such. That the Money Market factor in a Government Loan embodies and absorbs into itself the Political factor is evident from the fact that the tightness of money, which raises the rate of interest, is not so much due to the relation between the amount of money as such and the amount of products it distributes, as it is to the degree of general credit which exists at the time in relation to these products—as is proved by the fact that when markets are buoyant and general credit good, little money is necessary to effect the ordinary transactions of business, whereas when markets are suspicious and credit is bad much more money is required; and when, as in a panic, credit is for the time absolutely shattered, there is often not money enough in a whole country to carry out its necessary business transactions. And as it is the *credit* of a country which political troubles and complications affect, it is evident that the Political element is included in the Money Market element in any and every alteration of the rate of interest of a Government Loan.

But that the *amount of money* itself in the market is, in spite of this, a separate element in the total make-up of the market rate of interest, is seen in the fact that if the money floating in the market, or lying in the banks waiting for investment, has from any cause become depleted, and ready money in consequence is scarce, not only is the ordinary rate of discount high, but the interest demanded for the flotation of loans, Government or other, will be higher than it otherwise would be. And hence it is usual for the projectors of all large industrial enterprises, as well as of all new loans, to wait until these temporary periods of money depletion have passed.

But when a conjunction of circumstances has conspired to give this period of money depletion a permanent rather than a passing character, as when a destructive and barren war has absorbed many millions of a nation's money without reproductive return, then the rate of interest for loans remains high over long periods of years together; and while it lasts there is not a Corporation or Debenture Stock in the country which does not fall in value, however strongly it may be secured from an industrial point of view.

Carrying with us then the fact that a certain customary amount of money always on hand for loanable purposes is necessary as a basis or support for the credit on which a money market has been in the habit of conducting its transactions; and that if any considerable amount of this loan money is suddenly withdrawn from any cause, the national credit will suffer, and the rate of interest to be paid for loans will rise; we are led to the third factor which enters into the rate of interest to be paid for a Government Loan, viz., the Industrial Factor.

And this brings us to the point which we must now determine, namely, as to what relation the Money Market element (embodying and reflecting in itself, as it does, the Political element) bears to the Industrial or wealth-producing element in a Government Loan; or, to put it into other words, which has the greater effect on the rise or fall of the rate of interest of a Government Loan, and indirectly through that of all other Debentures and loans whether of Industries or Corporations—the Money Market factor, or the strictly Industrial and wealth-producing one.

To begin with, we may say that the Industrial status of a country— the amount of its accumulated wealth and the extent of its wealth-producing power—must ultimately determine its credit and the rate of interest it will have to pay for its loans; and so in the end must dominate all Money Market influences, precisely as does the amount of credit that will be given to an individual; excepting, perhaps, amid the chances of war.

But for all ordinary purposes of investment for stability and security, Money Market influences prevail over Industrial. But to get a general idea of the degree to which this is so, we must draw a line of division athwart the various stocks, a line which in a rough way will separate those of a public nature from those which are purely private concerns. The former, which comprise Government Stocks, have their fluctuations mainly determined by Politics and the Money Market, as we have already seen, as well as by the activity or otherwise of the dealings in them on the Stock Exchange, into which a large element of speculation must necessarily enter.

But it is precisely the same, it is to be observed, with all Loans and Debentures whatever; for however well secured their Industrial basis may be, their rates of interest take their points of departure from the

Government Loans; and if these have to pay a high rate of interest for any reason, the Industrial loans have to pay a still higher—higher, indeed, than would be justified by the actual Industrial element on which they rest, and higher than if they were located in countries whose Government loans could be floated on a lower rate of interest.

An Industrial Debenture in Japan, for example, would have to pay a higher rate of interest on precisely the same Industrial security than it would have to pay on the same security if situated in England; and that for no better reason than that the Government Loans of Japan have to pay a higher rate of interest than English Consols. And hence it is that in this margin of difference between the rates of interest on the Government Loans of the two countries, the prudent investor will find an opening to plant his capital in Industrial concerns of equal stability and security, but yielding a higher rate of interest in the one country than in the other.

Practically, we may say that the only stocks where the Industrial factor plays a more important part than the Money Market one, and where the ups and downs of their quotations follow more closely the published returns of the business done than they do the oscillations of the Money Market, are the Ordinary shares of private or Limited Liability Industrial and Commercial concerns; and then only when they are largely left to themselves, and not made the endless subject-matter of speculation by the public on the Stock Exchange.

Speaking generally, and in the large, we may say, too, that the stocks of all private companies whose industries have rich potentialities in them, but which are still undeveloped, are more dependent on the Money Market than on their actual Industrial and productive powers for their quotations on the Stock Exchange; whereas all industries that have reached their normal Industrial development will follow the Money Market influences as regards their loans, but (except when Stock

Exchange speculation is busy with them) will follow the published yields of their Industrial returns as regards their Ordinary shares.

From all the foregoing considerations taken together, then, we are obliged to conclude that as the Industrial and productive powers of a country are at bottom the only solid foundation for the permanent stability and security of its stocks, there are a number of nations in the world where the conditions are such that capital can be invested with equal practical stability and security, but with a greater yield of interest, than either in the stocks of any particular nation, or in the Government Stocks of all nations.

These conditions are found (1) in those nations where, owing to the high rate of interest which, from Political or Money Market causes, the Government Loans have to pay, many Corporation and private Industrial Loans of unimpeachable Industrial security are paying rates of interest far and away above those of loans no better secured in other countries; or (2) in the loans of innumerable private Industrial concerns, in all countries, which also are amply secured, but which change hands seldom, and are little quoted in Stock Exchange reports; or (3) in the loans of private or Corporation concerns in countries of great potential wealth, like Brazil or Argentina, still largely undeveloped, and where rates of interest, owing to the actual scarcity of money, are unusually high; or (4) in the loans, whether Corporation, Railway, or Industrial, of any country where law and order and the enforced payment of debts prevail; where the capital at the back of a loan is not largely "goodwill," but tangible property which in the event of a break-up of the business will in a forced sale repay both the capital and interest of the loan; and where solid business, and not Stock Exchange speculation, is the main basis for the fluctuations of its rise or fall. But all these principles require a definite practical scheme in which to give them a setting; and it is to a scheme of this kind that I would invite the reader's attention in the next chapter.

CHAPTER V.GEOGRAPHICAL DISTRIBUTION VERSUS INSURANCE

IN this chapter I have now to sum up this somewhat lengthy dissertation on Stocks, Money Markets, Exchanges, etc., with the object of ascertaining, if possible, whether some sound practical scheme of investment, with a definite code of guiding rules and principles as its embodiment, may not be constructed out of it all.

I am aware, of course, that amid so heterogeneous a diversity of principles, positions, and points of view as we have already discussed, it is impossible to find any one principle so central and commanding as to form the nucleus of a scientific scheme of investment, especially as so many of these principles are bound up with the risks and contingencies of a future which at best, especially in matters of business, can only be imperfectly foreseen. But this very impossibility itself suggests the hope that perhaps the opposite method may be more successful, viz., of leaving the separate heterogeneous principles standing as they are, each on its own independent footing and with its own special risks attached to it, and then treating the whole after the manner of an Insurance Company, where, by the application of the Law of Probabilities, the risks attaching to each can be made so to neutralise and balance each other that a solid deposit will be left over to the good. It is at bottom the old familiar method of getting rid of the business risks of any special concern by putting your investment eggs into different baskets; like the bookmakers who, by balancing a certain number of horses against each other and laying their bets accordingly, manage to make almost a scientific certainty out of a business where the most expert judgment of form and running is likely in the end to lead its possessor, if he relies on it entirely, into bankruptcy.

Now, I venture to believe that in some scheme of this kind will be found the solution of the Problem of Investment, provided always that you can either make the principles, methods, and conditions of your scheme of investment run on "all fours," as it were, with the condition of things which obtains in, and makes the success of, Insurance Companies; or, if this is not possible, that you can supply what is missing by something of equal if not greater precision and certainty. And, accordingly, it is to the resemblances and differences between the principles on which an Insurance Company is based, and those on which a Geographical Distribution of Capital relies, that I would now direct the reader's attention.

To begin with, then, I may remark that the different categories of risks into which the individual stocks and shares of a Geographical Distribution of Capital are thrown, are not only as definite in character as the categories of risks into which the miscellaneous lives of individual men are poured in a Life Insurance Company, but are more in number. Let us take them in order and follow them from point to point; bearing in mind always that it is the degree of definiteness and limitation that can be imposed on the separate factors of any complex problem that marks the extent to which our conclusions can be reduced to a scientific probability or certainty.

Now, the first and supreme limitation of all Insurance Companies, and the one which dominates all the rest, is the limitation in the length of human life in general. Were this two hundred years, or onwards to . the age of Methuselah himself, instead of practically some eighty or ninety years, the table of risks on which the law of averages and probabilities has to operate, and on which the success of Insurance Companies depends, would have to be reconstituted from top to bottom. Is there, then, anything corresponding to this, and having a parallel precision and definiteness, in any possible scheme of Geographical Distribution of Capital among the different nations of the world? Yes; and it is to be found in the *steady amount of trade* which is always being transacted in the world as a whole and which is continually being redistributed among the different nations. This trade not only remains steady as a whole, but, owing to the gradual increase of the population of the world, is, as statistics show, steadily rising in amount, giving the investor assurance that if it is declining in one region of the globe it will, like the atmosphere, be correspondingly heaped up in another; and so makes a universal depreciation or slump at any time in all the securities embraced in a Geographical Distribution of Capital impossible.

In this way the prudent investor gets the same kind of solid support for the balancing of his risks against each other in a Geographical Distribution of his Capital as is given in Insurance Companies by the general equality in the length of human life; and from this supreme certainty as we come down the scale, all the other categories of risks hang suspended, and have to be estimated in reference to it as their fixed point. But these other categories can not only be as strictly limited and defined in a Geographical Distribution of Capital as in a Life Insurance Company; there are also more of them for the investor to catch hold of, as it were, and so help himself to a more accurate forecast of the future of his investments.

In Life Insurance Companies, for example, there are a number of categories or divisions, into which the risks are distributed before the innumerable lives to be insured are poured into them wholesale. There are divisions into good, medium, indifferent, and bad "lives," and these are represented in the reports of the medical examiners of the Company by such complex conditions as the hereditary predisposition to disease of the applicant, his family longevity, his existing constitution, the nature of his business, whether dangerous or otherwise, the climate of the country he inhabits, and the like.

Now, corresponding to these definite divisions in Insurance risks, we have in a Geographical Distribution of Capital the parallel fact that the different classes of stocks—Government Stocks, Corporation Loans,

Industrial Monopolies, Banks and Insurance Companies, Railway Debentures, Industrial Debentures, and the like—also lie in a hierarchy, and have, as we saw in former chapters, different natural values attached to them. In themselves these natural divisions are quite as definite as the good, medium, bad, or indifferent categories of lives in Insurance Companies; but over and above these, we have in a Geographical Distribution of Capital a number of *definite points of principle*, which play through the natural values of the different stocks, and make their future course still more amenable to scientific calculation.

One of these is the definite effect which the Government Stocks of any given country have in raising or depressing the market value of *all* other stocks in the same country. Another, as we have seen in a former chapter, is the effect of *the state of the Money Market* of the country over the rise or fall of all the shares and stocks of that country, especially of those which, like Debentures, come into it for loans. Of the same nature, again, is the calculable effect on the present and future of these stocks, of the *activity or slackness of the Stock Exchanges* which control particular descriptions of stocks in the country in which they are mostly dealt in. Besides these, there are the definite effect of the *state of Trade* in one country on that of a country with which it directly deals, and the like.

Now, these all help to give definiteness to the elements of the problem involved in a Geographical Distribution of Capital among the stocks of different nations; and, so far, have a scientific advantage over the fewer, rougher, and vaguer categories of risks in Insurance Companies. But by themselves they are not enough to give Geographical Distribution an all-round advantage over Insurance Companies; and something more therefore is necessary. For Insurance Companies, as we have seen in a former chapter, rest frankly on the impersonal Law of Probabilities, and this is itself a tremendous asset in their favour. For, however crude and vague their divisions of risks may be, there can be no doubt that such as they are, when innumerable lives of men are flung into them pell-mell, as it were, the risks will work out in proportion to the numbers thrown in, with a great measure of scientific accuracy. Geographical Distribution of Capital, on the other hand, although a form of insurance, has none of that impersonal character which in Insurance Companies works out its scientific averages quite independently of the discretion and judgment of men in the selection or rejection of its individual units. Its separate lists would, even in the largest single investments, not comprise more than twenty or thirty separate items in different parts of the world; and these are not sufficient in number in any given case to allow the Law of Probabilities scope for exercise. It would require something nearer 2,000 different investments than twenty or thirty, to give the law a chance; and that is, of course, practically an impossibility. Besides, these few investments have, in the last resort, to be selected by some one individual's judgment; and this is to infringe the cardinal principle on which all Insurance Companies are based—the purely impersonal Law of Averages and Probabilities.

It is evident, therefore, that if the Geographical Distribution of Capital is to rival the steadiness and sureness of Insurance Companies as a principle of investment, it will have to make good its deficiency in this respect by some principle as good, if not better, to take its place; and the question is whether such a substitute is anywhere to be found. I think it is; but it is not a single principle, but rather the resultant of a complex of several separate but all-important facts and principles.

The first is the fact that whereas in Insurance Companies the lives when once assigned to their appropriate categories of risk cannot afterwards be thrown aside and replaced by others should they prove to be bad ones; in an ordinary investment list, although it may not consist of more than half a dozen or a dozen separate risks distributed among the whole number of geographical divisions, the stocks can be changed in each division for other stocks of the *same character and status* as often as there is any reason to suppose that any particular stock held has from misfortune, accident, new inventions, and discoveries, or what not, been threatened with the loss of its former status. This fact is reinforced by two principles of great importance which reduce the risks attaching to the small number of separate investments to a minimum, and so give to the investor not only equal stability and security, but a higher yield than the Insurance Companies will give him.

The first of these principles is that a Geographical Distribution of Capital will deal in nothing but the choicest cuts, as it were, of the shares in any investment, viz., in Loans, Debentures, and Preference shares only, all of which bear a fixed rate of interest and take precedence of the great mass of Ordinary shares. Indeed, in any scheme of Geographical Distribution aiming at stability and security, and professing at all to be scientific, all Ordinary shares (the characteristic of which is that they go up and down with the ever-changing caprices of the market) must be ruthlessly ruled out from the investment list. So that it comes virtually to this, that instead of dealing with what is practically impossible for any single investor, viz., a vast miscellany of shares of every description, chosen haphazard on the chance that, as in an Insurance Company, the law of averages will be able to bring out of them a stable and equable result; a Geographical Distribution of capital would allot to each investor only a comparatively small variety of stocks at any one time; but then these would be of the very highest value in point of stability and security, and by being distributed among those nations of the world which follow different Money Markets, are subject to different Trade Currents, and yield different rates of interest on practically equally good security, would be made to balance each other's fluctuations.

But how, it will be asked, are we to know that the stability and security of each of the few stocks selected are in themselves, as industrial business concerns—and quite apart from the Money Markets, the Trade Currents, and the Stock Exchanges which form the separate environment in which they function—how do we know that these are above reproach? The answer is, that we look to the published and audited balance-sheets of the industrial business concerns on which our investment list of Loans, Debentures, and Preference shares is based; and if we find that they have twice as much capital behind them as the amount of the debenture or loan; that they have had for a period of five or eight years, say, a steady income averaging three times as much as is necessary to pay the interest on the loan; that they have habitually in hand more liquid assets than are necessary to pay their current trade debts; and, besides, can show that in the event of a break-up sale there is sufficient tangible property left (and not merely goodwill) to repay the loan with interest in full;—then we can safely say that that Debenture stock, in any country where private property is fully protected by law, is a first-class investment stock, so far, that is to say, as its ultimate security is concerned.

With the real solidity of our investment list thus assured by the unimpeachable security of the *Industrial* basis on which each of the Loans, Debentures, and Preference shares rests, we can then proceed to place each of these solid securities in the special environment in which it functions; i.e., in the particular *country* in which it is situated; with the special *rate of interest* which that country has to pay on its Government Loans; in the particular *Stock Exchange* in which the bulk of its stock is held; and in the particular *Trade Currents,* as between country and country, in which its business is carried on.

This done, we can then divide the World up into sections, and group the different countries according to the kind of products which form the mainstay of their prosperity; keeping those which deal mainly in agricultural produce, fruit, raw materials, or what not, separate from each other and from those which are engaged in manufacturing and working up these products. These countries are then suspended in a circlet, as it were, around the circumference of the great wheel of World-industry, but so regrouped and rearranged on it by lines of cross-division as to keep the factors which we have to balance against each other in our investment list separate and independent of each other.

The first of these cross-divisions connects the countries which trade with each other and supply one another's wants, and so are reciprocally affected by one another's prosperity or adversity. The second of the cross-divisions connects the countries the bulk of whose shares are dealt with on the same Stock Exchange, as, for example, our Colonies and India, which have the London Stock Exchange for their centre, thus marking the effect of the Money Market on the loans and debentures of our investment list when these latter are otherwise adequately secured on their industrial side. The third of these cross-divisions connects the countries whose natural resources, like those, for instance, of Brazil and Argentina, are rich, but where the capital necessary for their development is insufficient, with others, like England, where capital is overflowing, but fresh openings for it at home are not forthcoming; thus marking the parts of the earth where loans on private industries—as distinct from Government or Corporation Loans—can be planted with the assurance of a high yield of interest. And the last cross-division, the one with the most universal and all-pervading importance, is between those countries whose Government Loans pay a high rate of interest and those which pay a medium or a low rate; for the Government rate of any particular country, like a higher or lower pitched key, will raise or depress the value of all stocks whatever in that country, even after Money Markets, Stock Exchanges, Trade Currents, and purely Industrial Security have produced each its own proper effect, and done its best or worst with them.

Here, then, is a complex of separate definite principles and conditions, playing into and around each particular stock of each and every country, and modifying the natural industrial or commercial value of each stock on an investment list. If, then, the industrial basis for the loans and debentures of our investment list is so fully secured as to be above suspicion or reproach, it is evident that we must depend for our average *yield of income* from them on the way in which we balance the influence of these various Trade Currents, Money Markets, Stock Exchanges, and Government Securities of the different countries against each other.

If this be accurately and skilfully done, there is no reason why the prudent investor should not be certain of getting a larger yield of income, with equal stability and security, from a Geographical Distribution of Capital than from any other mode of investment. It is thoroughly scientific in character, inasmuch as there is nothing haphazard in the selection of its list of stocks; and, besides, all the factors that enter into the problem can be sufficiently well known from day to day, month to month, and year to year, from the reports of Money Markets, Stock Exchanges, Trade Statistics, and Government Loans. For in the art with which it balances these factors of a few stocks against each other, it resembles rather, as I have said, the hedging of the scientific bookmaker than the averaging of the ordinary Insurance Companies.

Like the horses in a race, the number of stocks in an investment list are few in number; while the qualities of the horses, their past records and present form, the jockeys that ride them, the length of the course, the nature of the ground, etc., correspond to the past history and present quotations of the stocks, and to the Money Markets, Stock Exchanges, and Trade Currents which ride and dominate them. The weighing and combining of the points for or against the horses in order to determine the odds given or taken, and so to give balance and symmetry, stability and security to a book, depend on personal judgment and penetration; so, too, do the weighing and combining of the points for or against a stock, and the giving to this stock its proper place in the balance and symmetry of the investment list as a whole.

The problem of a scientific Geographical Distribution of Capital, in a word, is the problem of the scientific selection, by means of personal discretion and judgment, of a small number of stocks which, under conditions of great complexity, and an immense number of possible combinations, will balance each other's risks. In an ordinary Insurance Company, on the other hand, the problem is, how to pack into a small number of generalised categories of risks such a large number of miscellaneous lives, thrown helter-skelter in, as will neutralise each other's risks by their numbers alone, without the intervention of any further personal discretion or judgment in the matter. Of course, the more definite and accurate the categories of any classified risks, even of an Insurance Company, the better.

My point is that while Insurance Companies could almost dispense with all distinctions of risks whatever, provided they had mere gross numbers enough of lives to pour into them; a Geographical Distribution of Capital can only succeed in proportion to the discrimination, accuracy, and completeness with which each factor or element involved in the problem is separately analysed and grasped in relation to every other and to the whole.

Such, in bald outline, is a brief summary of the principles which, in my judgment, ought to preside over a Geographical Distribution of Capital; and before closing this already too lengthy dissertation it would be well to consider to what extent they have been embodied in any detailed existing scheme. The only one of which I have any cognisance is that of Mr. Henry Lowenfeld, as unfolded in his various books on Investments; a scheme the essentials of which were subsequently carried out by the late Sir Edward Law, when engaged in his capacity as director, in investing the huge surplus funds of one of our most important Insurance Companies. Personally, I am much indebted to Mr. Lowenfeld for being the first to suggest to me the various elements which, as a practical investor, he had found entering into the composition of share values, as well as into their mode of action; and for suggesting them to me as a proper subject for the Science of Finance.

I propose, therefore, to wind up this dissertation by giving an outline of his scheme; but before doing so I shall sum up Sir Edward Law's leading maxims in his own words, in order that the reader may have the opportunity of comparing the relative positions occupied on this problem of investment by a speculative economist like myself, on the one hand, and a practical financier on the other, and of observing how closely their conclusions coincide.

The first of Sir Edward Law's principles is that the stocks selected for an investment list should not all be confined to one market; the second is that the group of stocks selected should be distributed among different countries; the third, that they should belong to different categories; the fourth, that the total sum invested should be fairly equally divided among the various classes of stocks selected; the fifth, that the number of stocks selected should vary in proportion to the sum to be invested, and that the small investments should comprise at least four or five different categories of stock, the more ordinary of these categories comprising Government, Municipal, Railway, Shipping, Banks, and Industrial, the latter including in general terms not only Manufacturing Industries, but also Gas and Water Stocks, Harbour Trusts, Telegraphs and Telephones, etc.; the sixth, that each individual stock should offer good security in itself; and the seventh, that the past history of the stocks selected should show that the fluctuations of the individual securities have all kept approximately within the same limits of width of variation. And his conclusion is that "if all these conditions be fulfilled, whilst no guarantee can be given for the future of any particular stock, it is fairly certain that if some prove bad bargains, others will increase in value, and that the law of averages will assure a far more reliable collective result than any likely to be attained by the most careful selection of securities, based solely on apparent respective individual worth."

To these first principles of Sir Edward Law I can only add—what indeed must be evident from all I have already said on my own account—that I unhesitatingly subscribe. In the next chapter we will consider Mr. Lowenfeld's scheme.

CHAPTER VI.MR. LOWENFELD'S SCHEME

AFTER what I have already said in former chapters, the principles, maxims, and detailed application of Mr. Lowenfeld's scheme for the Geographical Distribution of Capital need not detain us long; for although his detailed exposition of them extends through several volumes, his leading principles are confined mainly to those I have discussed in my last chapter. I have thought, therefore, that it would simplify matters for the reader, as well as avoid needless repetition, if I arranged his materials in my own way, and kept as close as possible to the order of my own exposition in the last chapter. But I wish to say frankly at the outset that the credit of the scheme belongs to Mr. Lowenfeld and not to me; and that it was only when it had been submitted to me for an opinion, and after I had found myself essentially in agreement with it, that I undertook to take up the whole question from my own separate and independent point of view.

To begin with, then, I may remark that Mr. Lowenfeld approaches his problem in a strictly scientific spirit, and from the true Baconian standpoint, founding his generalisation on a wide induction from the particulars of actual transactions; and these generalisations he applies to the infinite complexities of trade through the medium of a large number of business maxims.

I am aware that the late Sir Edward Law enunciated the same principles as being those which guided him in his capacity as investor for a large Insurance Company, but Sir Edward Law's publications are subsequent to those of Mr. Lowenfeld and based upon what was already in print. In the meantime we may extract a few of Mr. Lowenfeld's principles and maxims with the view of giving the reader a taste of his quality as a financial expert. His principles are few in number. The largest in scope of these, and the one which, if scientifically established, forms the presupposition, axiom, or postulate of the rest, which hang on it and draw their vitality from it, is that the great trading countries of the world form themselves into different groups, each of which has an organising financial centre which, like the brain, dominates and controls the separate markets as well as the trading hopes, fears, and possibilities of the whole group. London, for example, as we saw in the last chapter, is the brain and Money Market centre for all British Trustee stocks; and although these have been lately extended to certain Indian and Canadian stocks, to the stocks of great Corporations, like the City of London, the London County Council, Belfast, Birmingham, and so on, as well as to the Inscribed stocks of our widely separated Colonies, they all rise or fall in value together—and quite independent of their intrinsic, ultimate, individual merits—according to the freedom or stringency of money in the London Money Market.

It is the same, too, with the Trade Currents as with the Money Markets of the world. They each have their separate geographical divisions, routes, and connections; and Mr. Lowenfeld's first object, accordingly, is to ascertain precisely what these geographical divisions are. He has succeeded in reducing them to ten, all told, viz., British, Colonial, North Europe, South Europe, Asia, Africa, North America, South America, and an International division representing International Trusts, Shipping, Telegraph, and Marine Insurance, etc. These major divisions he splits up, in turn, into subdivisions, with the object of more accurately marking out and separating the Money Market connections from the connections of the Trade Currents and of the Stock Exchanges. This done, he has then to show two things before he can launch his scheme. The first is, that the relative amount of trade done by these different divisions of the world collectively may be divided into two halves, as it were, which are *complementary* to one another; so that when the trade and monetary conditions of the one half are known, those of the other half may be roughly inferred. But that, again, can only hold good provided it can be shown that the trade of the world *as a whole* is a steady or slowly progressive one, and not capricious and variable. And this position Mr. Lowenfeld finds verified in the statistics compiled with much care and accuracy by Mr. Holt Schooling.

It will be as well therefore, if we are to rightly apprehend Mr. Lowenfeld's position, to pause for a moment to consider what these conclusions of Mr. Schooling specially are, and what further conclusions can logically be drawn from them. They may be summed up, then, in the following propositions: (1) That the trade of the world as a whole, owing to the increase of population and the mouths that have to be fed, is steadily increasing; (2) that it has compensatory fluctuations as between Europe and the rest of the world; (3) that the exports of Europe are two-thirds of those of the whole world; (4) that the share of European exports is gradually falling; (5) that as far as Europe and the whole of America is concerned, the share of exports is falling in the former and rising in the latter; (6) that Europe as a whole has largely increased her export trade, but that the United Kingdom has not kept up to the rest of the world in this respect; and lastly, and as conclusion and summary of the whole, that although fluctuation in the amount of trade characterises the different parts of the world, the world as a whole is free from fluctuation.

Now, if these propositions be true, two things must follow. The first is that the price paid for loans of capital will vary according to the wealth and credit of the different countries of the world; the second is embodied in a maxim of Mr. Lowenfeld's, viz., that "no circumstances can cause all the stocks of a Geographical Distribution to show a simultaneous depreciation below cost price"; and putting these two propositions together, he concludes that if an investor will take the pains to separate the parts played in the price of the stocks in different countries by the Money Markets that dominate them, and by the Trade Currents that blow through them and stimulate or depress them, he will be able to hold with safety stocks yielding a larger income than he otherwise could do. And in testing this on a typical all-British list of investments, and a typical geographically distributed one respectively, it was found (1) that the geographically distributed one produced twenty per cent more income than the all-British one from the beginning; (2) that the all-British one improved in value £2,902 during the first five years, but ended in a loss of £137; (3) that the geographically distributed one rose gradually in volume but maintained its value, and finally increased it by £1,524; and lastly, that while the annual income from both lists followed the rise of capital, the £2,902 rise in the all-British capital ended only in an increase of income of £54, whereas in the rise of £1,524 in the geographically distributed one the rise in capital value was attended by a proportionate rise of income.

But not to depend upon particular figures or particular selections of stocks for our comparison, it would be as well, perhaps, if we could find in Mr. Holt Schooling's statistics of World-trade some inherent reason why, at the present stage of industrial development, a Geographical Distribution of Capital will secure a larger yield of income, with equal stability and security, than any mode of investment in the stocks of any single country. The principle of averaging, or not putting all your eggs in one basket, might of course account for a large measure of stability and security, but it could not account for the greater yield, except on the condition that money must essentially yield a higher rate of interest, on equal security, in some countries than in others; whereas, to invest entirely in the stocks of the particular country which pays the highest rate of interest on its loans, would be to sacrifice the stability and security of our investments to the pretensions of their face value. If, on the other hand, we go to the opposite extreme, and put all our capital into Consols and other British Government Stocks paying the lowest rate of interest, for the sake of *ultimate* security, we sacrifice a larger possible yield and an equal *practical* security; and without attaining to any higher degree of stability, owing to the greater dependence of

Government Stocks on political and international complications than other stocks; as, indeed, the fluctuations of Consols during the last twenty years have abundantly shown.

Or, again, it may be suggested that if we limited our capital for investment entirely to the Government Stocks of the *different* countries, it would meet all the conditions of our problem, viz., a higher average yield, owing to the difference in the rates of interest in these various Government Stocks; and a greater stability and security, owing to the eggs not being all in the same basket. But in this it is forgotten that there are not sufficient Government Stocks in the world to give the law of averages and probabilities a chance to operate, inasmuch as all the Government Stocks of a particular country count only as one stock, owing to their all having the same security. But Mr. Lowenfeld's scheme avoids this difficulty by means of two devices.

In the first place he limits severely the amount of money appropriated to Government Stocks in any single investment list—not more than a fourth of the whole, if I remember rightly, and even that only because in the event of any necessity arising when ready money must be had immediately, they can be converted into it with both cheapness and ease. Indeed, were it not for the necessity of having some part of an investment list in a fluid, quickly convertible form, it is probable that, owing to the instability which political and international complications are apt to produce in Government Stocks (but from which Industrial Debentures and Loans, as we saw in a former chapter, are comparatively free), he would confine his investment lists to Corporation Loans, Railway and Industrial Debentures and Preference Stocks entirely, and eschew Government Stocks almost as much as he does Ordinary shares. For these Debentures and Industrial shares, as we saw, are the last to be disturbed by political or social commotions; and, what is more important in this connection, there are hundreds or thousands of them, and of the most unimpeachable security, from which to make a choice, in every country of the world. And the consequence of this is, that should any one or more of them fail through accident or unforeseeable misfortune, there always remains any number of them to draw from, with which to fill the gap in an investment list; thus giving a sufficient number and variety for the law of averages to take effect in.

Besides, no inherently weak or risky Industrial stocks are admitted into Mr. Lowenfeld's lists. In his scheme, on the contrary, each stock selected is in itself of unimpeachable security, and if it cannot pass his test is not admitted. These stocks consist, as I have said, mainly of Loans and Debentures and Preference shares; and the conditions which he has laid down as essential before they can be admitted to his lists, are (1) that they shall be based on the security of business concerns which have had for five or more years a steady income averaging three times as much as is necessary to pay the interest on the Debenture or Loan; (2) that they shall have twice as much capital behind them as the amount of this Debenture or Loan; (3) that they shall have habitually on hand more liquid assets than are necessary to pay the current trade debts; and (4) that in the event of a break-up sale from accident or misfortune, they shall have sufficient actual tangible property left to pay the loan with interest in full.

In my last chapter I accepted these conditions of Mr. Lowenfeld's as sufficient to justify an investor in holding a stock as a permanent investment and embodied them in my own rough outline of what an investment scheme on the lines of Geographical Distribution should be.

Now, with all the stocks in his investment lists equally well secured on the Industrial side, it is natural that Mr. Lowenfeld should look to the other factors that enter into the value of stocks for the differentiation necessary to give him that high average of yield, with equal security and stability, which he claims for his scheme. And, indeed, this is precisely what he does. He argues that the main causes of this differentiation in yield are the prices of the Government Stocks of the different countries on the one hand, and the influence of the different Stock Exchanges in which particular classes of stock are dealt in; the separate and distinct Trade Currents that flow between different countries; and the stringency or ease of their Money Markets on the other. But of all these the influence of the price of Government Stock is paramount, inasmuch as it affects all the stocks of a country, and is more permanent, whereas that of Stock Exchanges, Trade Currents, and Money Markets, is more partial, more casual, more transient, and more fluctuating.

Now, it will have been observed that, although Mr. Lowenfeld has relied mainly on the difference in price of Government Stocks for giving him in his scheme of Geographical Distribution the different rates of yield from which to get a higher average on equally good security than from other modes of investment, he makes his selection not from the Government Stocks themselves of the different countries, but from the Loans, Railway and Industrial Debentures or Preference shares of these countries. The reason is that as the latter are all equally affected by the prices of their respective Government Stocks they offer the same differentiations from which to strike an average as the Government Stocks themselves; but have these further advantages over Government Stocks, that they return a greater yield of interest; enjoy equal practical security; and (what is equally important for an investor) are freer from fluctuation. They yield a greater percentage of interest, not so much because Government Stocks are more ideally secure, and so have to pay less for a loan, but because, like money in one's pocket or on deposit in a bank, you can turn them into cash at any time, or at any place in their own country, with the least expense, the least delay, and the greatest ease. They are more free from fluctuation because, as we have already seen, they are less influenced by *political* or *international* complications and disturbances than Government Stocks necessarily are.

Later on I will present the reader with some of the maxims Mr. Lowenfeld lays down in reference to the effects of Stock Exchanges, Trade Currents, and Money Markets, on the current prices, if not the inherent ultimate value, of different geographical securities; but before doing so we may pause for a moment to consider some of the causes which have made the Government Stocks of some countries of so much lower credit for stability and security than those of others; and, in consequence, make it necessary for the industrial enterprises of these countries, however safely secured, to pay a higher rate of interest for loans. The causes, of course, are political and social as well as industrial in character. They include such considerations as the political stability or instability of the country in question; its freedom or not from either the dangers of internal revolutions or of external complications with other Powers; the stability of its Money standard, and of the laws of property and taxation; the honour of the country as a whole, or of its Municipalities and Corporations, in meeting or repudiating their debts, etc.

On the other hand, the credit of a country and the price it has to pay on its loans may be mainly *industrial* in character, and depend on such causes as the natural productive powers of the country, whether in its soil, its mines, or its facilities of communication and transport, the number of natural monopolies it possesses, either in the quality of the foodstuffs or fruits, in its metals or precious stones, its furs or timber, its rubber or ivory, or what not; or, again, on the inventive or energising ability of the people, their scientific knowledge and its application to machinery and to all the arts that minister either to the necessities or luxuries of life. Or again, the credit of a country (as reflected in the rate of interest of its loans) may depend on the amount of the existing indebtedness of the country as a whole, and of its municipalities and corporations; the proportion of these loans which has been spent on reproductive works, and the proportion which has been either blown away in fruitless military expenditure or in paying off old debts, in political corruption, etc. Summing up, then, these various causes which in their combination determine the relative rates of interest which different Governments have to pay on their loans, and dividing them broadly into the relative amount of *productive industrial power* which they possess, on the one hand, and the relative amount of debt which these industrial powers have to carry, on the other, we may tarry for a moment on our way with the object of considering their *modus operandi* as preliminary to the maxims of Mr. Lowenfeld in regard to them, which are to follow.

The first point I would mention is, that the mere gross amount of a nation's *debt* will by itself give us no true or final indication of its *credit*, but only when taken in relation to its *productive powers,* present or prospective—to its present productive powers in the case of short-period investments, and to its prospective productive powers in the case of the long-period ones with which Mr. Lowenfeld's scheme deals. It is not every debt that benumbs or strangles either the individuals of a nation or the nation itself. Some debts are the sole means of opening up the hidden resources of a country or of developing them still further, and so are a blessing in disguise. It is only when the capital borrowed is sown on a stony, barren soil, productively speaking, that the debt becomes an incubus on production; if it falls on a rich soil, it waters and increases it like a fertilising rain. If the debt then, however great in itself, is light compared with the wealth-producing Powers of Nature which the capital of the debt can evoke, whether from the soil, as in the improvements of agriculture, or from the use of machinery in manufactures—it adds to wealth production; if, on the contrary, the weight of the floating balloon of debt, like a hydrocephalic head, is too heavy for the wealth-producing Powers of Nature which have to carry it as a going concern, when its products are put on the market at the existing market price, then it becomes top-heavy "over-capitalised" as they say—and staggers and tumbles into bankruptcy, with the loss of all the stored-up human labour which the capital of the debt represented.

It is precisely the same with National Debts as it is with the debts contracted by individual traders, Joint Stock Industrial Companies, or Corporations; but with this difference, that whereas the chances are that individual traders will employ the capital of their debt productively; and with Joint Stock Companies, as things at present go, it is perhaps about even chances as to whether it is productively or unproductively spent; and while Corporations, again, will spend their borrowed capital productively on the whole, even when they are paying more for the work on which they employ it than is necessary, or than would be paid for it were it in private hands; Governments, it is most probable (except, perhaps, in the case of a fight for their very existence), will spend most of their borrowed capital un-productively, in military establishments, in wars, etc.; while they are only beginning to learn the importance of spending it in industrial enterprises which are beyond the resources of any individual or Joint Stock Company.

Again, very few nations, as such, have any *public* property at all as security for their debts (except, perhaps, Germany, whose debts are secured on a network of railways and canals owned by the State), but have to depend almost entirely on the taxes which they can squeeze out of their subjects. And however equally these taxes may be laid on the different classes of a nation, it is evident that if they exceed a certain amount, and the capitalist class cannot shift their share on to the shoulders of the general public, the nation itself in its industrial rivalry with other nations must go under in the struggle for existence; so long, that is to say, as the present industrial organisation of society lasts.

All this is, of course, trite, but it leads up to a point of more importance, viz., why it is that the fortunes of the capitalist class should be so much more bound up and identified with the fortunes of the nation as a whole than those of the other classes. The answer is, that it is from the *Powers of Nature* that the accumulating surplus of wealth which gives nations their status and credit comes—and not from the hands, backs, and shoulders of men. And it is the capitalist class, it must be remembered, which owns the machines and processes which make this surplus—not the working classes. Without the machines, indeed, these would, if left to rely on their own resources, "eat their heads off," however great their numbers might be; and, moreover, not one in ten thousand of them could invent a machine, or part of one, if they tried.

It is true that the Capitalist for the most part exploits and skins the Inventor on whom he is dependent for the machines and processes by which he is enabled to add to the surplus of wealth of the world; and that the greatly successful inventor, who is one in a million, may come from any class. Still, as things are at present, it is the capitalist class which represents the new inventions and processes, without which no nation can hold its own in the race for wealth; and hence it is that Capital, which brings to both the *machines*, which in turn capture and enchain the *Powers of Nature*, which in their turn, again, give a surplus of wealth to a nation over and above the labour spent on them; it is Capital that in the end, through this accumulating surplus, gives a nation its financial *credit and status* among the other nations. In other words, it is its Capital—and not the number of its inhabitants, nor the natural riches of its undeveloped soil or mines—which gives a nation the power of exploiting the wealth of other nations in every deal between them. For just as gold is the crown and ultimate object of all hearts, as being the sole final representative of wealth, and so discounts all other commodities in any exchange between them; so, too, does Capital, the representative of gold, take a share off all other commodities in building up the wealth of nations. It can command the ownership and services of every wealth-producing machine, but no wealth-producing machine can be sure of commanding it.

If, then, we take Mr. Schooling's estimate that two-thirds of the trade of the world is done by Europe, while only one-third is done by all the world beside—and that, too, in spite of the fact that from time immemorial neither the number of its inhabitants nor the potential riches either of its soil or mines are a tithe of that of the rest of the world—we shall not go wrong if we conclude that it is the Capital of Europe which has done it, under the guidance of science, invention, and knowledge applied to the arts of life. But this Capital had to be accumulated by Europe first; and how this was done we have now to see.

In general terms we may say that it was because they had got the gods—the Machines, viz., which evoke the wealth-producing Powers of Nature—on their side; for these are the big battalions which in the end conquer in Trade, as in War; the mere Workers, like the opposing camps of Greeks and Trojans, being "much of a muchness" without their aid. It is not because the Eastern and Southern nations of the world have been denied the wealth-producing Powers of Nature which characterise its Northern and Western divisions, that little Europe has managed to capture two-thirds of the trade of the world. On the contrary, as I have said, they have been more richly endowed by Nature with mines, and fruits, and fertile soils, than Europe. It is rather because men are led by their imaginations the world over, and not by their mere stomachs, that they will sacrifice all they have above what is necessary for the mere sustenance of life for what will give them those symbols of distinction, honour, and prestige among their fellows, which they so dearly prize; and that among rude tribes, primitive peoples, and the great mass of mankind everywhere, these symbols are the products of Machinery—cheap gewgaws, ornaments for the person, coloured calicoes, flashy jewellery, and what not—turned out by the gross with the smallest expenditure of labour; and for which whole cargoes of natural products—corn, wine, figs, bananas, oranges, tea, coffee, and all that ministers to the bodily appetite—will be given, to feed the starving, swelling millions of the European slums.

On the other hand, the most God-forsaken regions of the other continents will erect themselves into wealthy States on the basis of the luxuries with which they feed the ostentation and vanities of the European rich—in one geographical division, sunburnt ostrich farms, or gold and diamond mines in barren ravines or dried-up water-courses and rocky hillsides, in another snow-covered wastes and the fur-yielding animals that roam over them. And the consequence is, that when objects of *imaginative desire and luxury* are pitted for exchange against mere *bodily necessities,* the nations that own the former, and the machinery which turns them out, as well as the nations that have a monopoly of the luxuries of the rich, will take the cream in every bargain between themselves and the nations that produce the mere gross raw materials which minister only to the bodily necessities of life. And it is because Europeans have all along supplied the world with the *artificial* products which minister to the imaginations of men, rather than with the food or fruit necessary for bodily sustenance, that they have got the best of the bargain in every exchange; and so have been enabled to accumulate that preponderating share in the capital, wealth, and trade of the world on which Mr. Schooling dwells.

In the Middle Ages, Venice, Florence, Genoa, and the other great trading cities of Italy, got it by being the middlemen through whose hands the produce both of the East and West had to pass before it could find its customers; and so were able to retain the lion's share of the profits for themselves. In later times, the European nations in turn—Spain, Portugal, Holland, and England—exploited the wealth of the East and West on their own account; and by their swords made themselves not only the distributing middlemen, but the owners as well of a great part of the lands of the East; thus still further adding to the capital, wealth, credit, and trade, of Europe as against the rest of the world. In the present day, the exploiting of the Eastern and Southern nations by the Western and Northern is no longer mainly done in their capacity as middlemen *taking toll,* nor yet as conquerors by *expropriation,* but chiefly by *loaning* them the capital back again which their trading positions and swords had been the means originally of extracting from them. Now, while Europe acted as middleman and took toll from the East, the East always got something in return; and when she acted as conqueror, and expropriated the wealth of the East, the latter got little or nothing in return; but now that she is acting as capital-supplier mainly, what is likely to be the result?

This is the question, bearing on Mr. Lowenfeld's scheme, to which I have all along been leading up. And the first thing that occurs to one is that in being freely supplied by European capital, the Eastern countries are gradually being equipped on their own soil with all the machinery and processes for the production, transmission, and distribution of all the wealth of which they are capable; and that although at first most of the profits of these concerns go to the European, still, with the instruments of production planted *on their own soils,* it needs must be that sufficient of this wealth created in their midst must in time filter through to themselves; and so in the end enable them to pay off their indebtedness, and own their railways, machinery, and plant themselves—precisely as happened with the United States of America under similar circumstances. And what this means in plain English is simply this—that as the rest of the world is richer in the *natural instruments* of wealth than Europe—in corn- and fruit-lands, in mines, etc., and in no long time will either own the *artificial instruments* of production in the shape of machinery and processes necessary to extract this wealth, or will have been taught how to make these instruments themselves, it is evident that in a comparatively few years, at the rate at which things are now going, Europe and the rest of the world will change places in the relative amount of trade and wealth-production with which they are credited by Mr. Schooling; and that instead of Europe doing two-thirds of the trade of the world and the rest of the world one-third, she will more likely do only the one-third while the rest of the world takes the two-thirds.

Now, Mr. Lowenfeld has in his scheme of the Geographical Distribution of Capital provided for its keeping step with this steady movement of the balance of trade from Europe and the West to the South and East, by confining his investment list not only to such stocks in each division of the world as are of unexceptionable security, but by insisting that the permanency not only of any particular investment in its own geographical division, but that of any particular geographical division itself, shall be only relative—in the sense, that is to say, that it shall keep time, as it were, to this general movement of wealth and trade from West to East, and be altered and rearranged at intervals accordingly. But the fact that the evolution is so slow and its stages so well marked gives the periodical changes in his investment list— changes which are made neither at too long intervals nor at too short ones—*a peculiar appropriateness*, differing in this markedly from a Life Insurance Company, for example, which when it once takes a risk has to carry it through to the end, even were all its clients to die on the morrow.

Summing up, then, this part of Mr. Lowenfeld's scheme dealing with the effects on a Geographical Distribution of Capital of its most potent and important regulator, viz., the different rates of interest paid by the different Government Loans of the different nations, and the different yields of income that may be got from investments in them according to the skill with which, as on a chess-board, they are played off against each other; we may say (1) that it is the difference in the yields of the Government Stocks of different nations that enables him to get a higher average interest, with equal practical security, and greater stability, than he could otherwise do; (2) that this average yield is raised still higher by the investments being made, not in Government Stocks themselves, but in Loans, Debentures, and Preference shares of the different nations instead, all of which pay higher rates of interest than their own Government Stocks, and, being more free from political and international influences, are more steady and less fluctuating; while, of course, preserving all the while the same relative position to each other as the different Government Stocks themselves do, and thus keeping the harmony of the whole unimpaired; and (3) that by permitting of periodical changes in the stocks held—whether these changes are from one stock to another in the same geographical division, or from one geographical division to another—the investment list can keep time, measure, and pace with the more permanent fluctuations of wealth and trade in the different divisions of the world.

Turning from the part played in Mr. Lowenfeld's scheme of Geographical Investment by the rate of interest of Government Loans, and their effect on all the other stocks in the same country, we have now to say something on that part of his scheme which deals with the influence of Stock Exchanges, Trade Currents, and Money Markets, all of which, although exercising in their aggregate a continuous, unceasing influence on the value of stocks, have, when each is taken separately, a transient and intermittent influence only on the changes that take place in their quotations; each when it has exhausted itself being taken up by one of the others, like that torch of learning which the ancients figured as being passed on without a break from hand to hand continuously. I have said so much on my own account in the previous chapters as to the effects of Money Markets, Stock Exchanges, and Trade Currents on the value of stocks, that it would be a supererogation to repeat it again here. It will be sufficient if I say, in general terms, that trade currents between particular countries affect the price of their stocks, inasmuch as a blow to the trade of one reacts on the trade of the others that deal with it, and so they suffer all alike. The temporary ease or stringency of the Money Market of a particular country again raises or depresses for the time being all the stocks of that country; so, too, the Stock Exchange in which a particular stock is mainly dealt in, whether situated at home or abroad, necessarily dominates the price of that stock, and for the time being elevates it above or depresses it below its inherent natural worth; while an Industrial stock that does not often change hands, but is far removed from the haunts of Stock Exchange operators, and is rarely quoted in the Stock Markets, is, if otherwise sufficiently secured, freer from fluctuation, and sounder for an investment which is to be permanent, than many a gilt-edged security with loftier pretensions. And I am given to understand by those who are in the business—what I otherwise should have doubted—viz., that a sound stock of this kind need never want for a ready purchaser.

Now, the way in which these Stock Exchange, Money Market, and Trade influences override the *natural and intrinsic values* of stocks is known to no one better than to Mr. Lowenfeld; and he has digested it into two leading maxims or aphorisms which bring out his sense of its deep importance. The first is, that "it is the value of the money which purchases stocks that varies"; and the second is, "that it is on the value of money that the international standard of investments depends." He is aware, of course, that a nation's *industrial* productivity or barrenness determines *in the long run* the relative position which its Money Market will take among the nations of the world; but he sees equally clearly that, for the comparatively limited term of years during which a stock held for investment may be expected to run, the state of the National Money Market overrides the Industrial productivity of the National resources. For it will be remembered that he limits his scheme of investment to jealously safeguarding the security of the capital invested, and confining its investment to the highest rate of interest compatible with that (viz., 4½ per cent or 5½ per cent, according to the amount of it which can be realised a*t any moment when it may he wanted, without loss*); and, further, that it is only Bonds, Debentures, and Preference shares that can fulfil these conditions of capital security with the greatest possible income. And as these (unlike Ordinary shares, which are mainly the subject-matter for speculation on their probable *industrial* yield) make their appeal in the first instance to the Money Market for loans, it is evident that he is right in making *the value of money* the primary and immediate, if not the ultimate controlling factor, in his scheme of Geographical Distribution.

As for Ordinary and Deferred shares, it is one of his maxims that these, in a case of permanent investment, should be eschewed altogether. But if the investor is determined to have a "flutter" in them on his own account, Mr. Lowenfeld hedges him round with all kinds of safeguards. He tells him to "watch the history of a stock and its fluctuations over a period of years"; to "avoid all stocks with a wide range of fluctuation, except Preference shares"; to select those stocks that are little known, and so are not influenced by newspaper and Stock Exchange rumour"; to see to it that the balancesheet of the stock in question shows, what I have already quoted, "three times as much capital behind a stock as in front of it; three times as much earnings as the interest which it has to pay on its Debentures"; and that "its liquid assets are greater than its current liabilities"; that "for capital stability the present value ought to be the basis of all reckoning"; and (for the novice) that "the yield of the stock should not be calculated on the cost." He points out, too, to all and sundry, whether they are speculators or investors, that "solid new issues never get their proper value"; and that, "irrespective of income, stocks with a minimum range of fluctuation and which rarely change hands are preferable." As for high rates of interest, he insists that "they do not *necessarily* mean insecurity, but only that most failures have been connected with them"; and that it is only in the case of *loan money* that a high rate of interest is insecure, not in that of well-grounded working concerns." Indeed, he goes so far as to say that "in a country where money is dear, even a first-class 6 per cent Debenture is good for ordinary investment purposes."

After preparing the reader with general maxims like the above, and starting with the preconception established by Mr. Schooling that the wealth of *the world as a whole* is steady, indeed is gradually increasing, and that it is only that of the *parts* which fluctuates—a preconception from which Mr. Lowenfeld draws the conclusion that "no set of circumstances can cause all the stocks of a Geographical Distribution to show a simultaneous depression below cost price"—he ushers his scheme on the stage by boldly applying what he calls the three "golden rules" of his system of investment to the ten geographical regions (with their various subdivisions) into which, for investment purposes, he has divided up the world.

The first of these rules is, to put the *same amount of capital* into each of the ten geographical divisions when the amount of the capital to be invested reaches, say, £1,000, and into fewer if the amount is less; while if the sum to be invested is a very large one, say £20,000 or £30,000, to put into subdivisions up to the extent of twenty or more.

The second rule is, to confine these equally divided amounts, thus distributed over different geographical areas, mainly to Corporation Loans, Railway and Industrial Debentures, and Preference Shares, showing *the same width of fluctuation* (and the narrower the better) over a considerable number of years. This is an important rule, and he hedges it round with a number of special observations bearing on the subject. One of them gives us the hint as to why he rules out Government Stocks largely from his lists; it is, that they fluctuate more violently than any other stocks, owing to the freedom and ease with which they change hands, as well as to their liability to become depressed in every political crisis whether of a temporary or a permanent nature; and he adds, quite justly, that they are also apt to remain depressed, owing to their low rate of interest, even when trade and enterprise are booming. And from this we see the reason of a remark he makes in another place, viz., that "the best Industrial Debentures are, as a rule, stable compared with Government Stocks."

Besides, it is a fallacy, he contends, to require a market as free for all your list of stocks as is the market for Government Stocks, inasmuch as good stocks, "as every stockbroker can tell you," are always saleable. Indeed, not more than a fourth of your investment list need be in Government Stocks, and that "only where prompt realisation for some passing emergency is required." And the upshot of it all is, that if you keep your eye on the past history of a stock, "it were better to select little-known securities not influenced by newspaper publicity and the consequent fluctuation of a free market." As for the rest, "it matters not which Money Market of the world controls a stock, so long as it pays to hold it at net cost, including all charges."

As regards the *width of fluctuation* that is permissible among the stocks in an investment list, he insists on two points; the first is "never to mix a 3 per cent fluctuation of yield with a 20 per cent one," and the second, "not to hold on to any stock which is already too high for safety." And to mark off his own Insurance scheme for the averaging of risks from all others professing to have the same object, he says that "by choosing a list of investments in which high and low yields, wide and narrow ranges of fluctuation, sound Debentures and speculative Ordinary shares are all mixed together, you do not get a true average, in the proper sense of the term, but only a false one, however wide a geographical distribution you make of them."

The third and last of Mr. Lowenf eld's rules for investment is, that each stock in a scientifically distributed list should be located in a country which follows entirely distinct Trade movements and influences, and is dominated by different Money Markets and Stock Exchanges from every other. This obliges the investor to keep his eye, like a skilful conjurer with his balls, on many Countries, Money Markets, Stock Exchanges, and Industrial conditions, at once; on the country where the majority of the stock is held, and whose Money Market, in consequence, is the dominant influence in its price quotations; on the price of Government Stocks in the country in which this particular stock is held, as that affects all the stocks; as well as on the balance-sheets of the concern, in which can be read the industrial basis for the loan if it is a private concern, or the rateable value of a municipality if it is a Corporation Loan. For were the investor to keep his eye only on the Money Market which controls the stock in question, he would be liable to see the property depreciate by *political* causes over which his Money Market has no control; on the other hand, were he to keep it only on the Industrial side of his investment, he would be apt to find it raided and depressed either from the influence of a distant Money Market, or from pure Stock Exchange speculation on his own market, however prosperous the concern in itself might be on its Industrial side.

So that if we picture Mr. Lowenfeld's scheme of investment as a kind of tape measure in which each division, according to his first maxim, contains the same length, or amount, of capital as every other; and, according to his second maxim, is of the same width as every other in its capital security and range of fluctuation, we can now, according to his third maxim, represent each division as being of a different colour from all the rest, inasmuch as it represents an entirely different Money Market, Stock Exchange, or Trade influence; these three constituting his "golden rule," and being summed up by himself in the dictum, that "safety of capital is obtained by its even division over a number of sound stocks identical in fluctuation, and every stock held subject to an entirely different Market influence." And with this he ends his dissertation, in the conviction that his scheme of Geographical Distribution on the principle of Insurance is the true one, and that he has scientifically solved the problem with which he set out, viz., of how to get the greatest income possible from investments compatible with the least range of fluctuation, and the complete security of the capital involved.

In the smaller complications that arise he has always some principle or maxim at hand with which to meet them. As regards British Trustee Stocks, he says frankly that "as they are all controlled by the same Money Market, and fluctuate greatly, they have not that capital stability which Trust funds should possess, owing to their being too much under the influence of the trade stagnation or prosperity of a single country." And hence if he had to make a choice between a Canadian Government 3 per cent Stock which as a Trustee Stock follows the low Money Market for loans in Britain, and a Canadian Local Stock adequately secured, but which follows the higher Money Market or different Trade influences of Canada herself—as indeed many first-class private or Corporation Stocks, Canadian Railroads, Hudson's Bay, and others do—and so have a higher yield, he would choose the latter for one division of his investment list, and not the former. And the difference in the value of money in the two countries leads him to the general observation that when reading the Money Article in the newspapers we should read it mainly to find out the "general movement in the value of money." Or, in other words, "The Money Article is a general indication of the rates of interest stocks should produce, and not of the fluctuations of individual investments."

"If, for example, Japanese Government Securities have risen five points, that means that Japanese Government Docks and Waterworks are likely to rise to a similar extent; or if the general rate of discount in Brazil has gone back, then local investments have gone up in value"; on the ground, I presume, as he elsewhere expresses it, that "the spending power of the people of a country is the dominating force which controls the realisable values of all stocks principally held in any one country." And he instances, in this connection, the case of the Taff Vale Railway, "whose dividends steadily increased, while the price of its stock declined."

So much, then, for the relative yield of different stocks. As for their relative width of fluctuation, he says that "in England few stocks are stable; but in France, Germany, Holland, Sweden, Norway, and even the United States, there are many. The fluctuation of first-class stocks in England ranges between twenty-five and forty points, in the other countries only between five and ten." This is important, and personally, on this ground, I should prefer to see more stocks invested in the European division perhaps than Mr. Lowenfeld is disposed to allow; but it is questionable whether they would not follow too closely the general European trade influence to get the advantage of an Insurance average, and whether the income from them would be sufficiently large, in spite of their otherwise greater security, to justify it. Incidentally, he remarks, apropos of the effect of different *Money Markets* on the price of stock, that a 4 per cent Debenture in England would yield 5 per cent in Africa on the same security.

On the other hand, as an example of the effect of different Trade movements on the price of stocks, he points out that Canada and India are unlike Australia (although they are all alike dominated by the same British Money Market); and that Belgium and Switzerland are also unlike, although they lie so close together.

Again, as bearing on his advice to sell out any stock when its price has risen too high for security, he says that there are two causes for a rise in stocks. The first is their improved intrinsic merits: this is a legitimate cause; but another cause equally potent is when some individual or group of individuals of great financial influence and authority announce that the future of the stock is bright: this is an illegitimate cause, and is the reason why many stocks go up too high for security.

As for downright bad stocks, he says that "the loss through them would pay the National Debt in four years, in spite of the work given to builders and their workmen, which cannot compensate to any degree for the loss of the capital involved." He makes also a very necessary distinction between the *internal* causes that affect a stock and the *external* ones; and he affirms that of all the internal causes, which consist either of competition, mismanagement, or bad organisation (and which are four times as strong as the external causes in all old well-tried investments), the holders of the stock get ample warning. It is only in new ventures that the alterations in capital safety, in management, and in dividend-earning power, have a great influence on a stock; but even then, after the stock has settled down, the internal influences, he repeats, again prevail.

I might extend these remarks of Mr. Lowenfeld indefinitely had I the space, but enough will have been given to send the reader to his various books on Investment themselves. But I may perhaps add, before closing, that Mr. Lowenfeld asks the investors who have accepted his scheme to "carry it into effect by spreading out the map of the World before them and putting a pin in at 1, London; 2, San Francisco; 3, Tokio; 4, Cape Town; 5, Melbourne; 6, Mid-Atlantic (for shipping insurance, cables, etc.); 7, Europe (Italy, say); 8, North America; 9, South America (Buenos Ayres); 10, Europe North and South, with a pin at Berlin; 11, Central America (with the pin in the centre of Mexico)." He then advises them "if the stock of the Italy pin, say, is above cost price the investor should sell it out and put it in an Austrian stock instead, if that country has credit below the normal. Or if the stock of Buenos Ayres is too high he should put it into that of Valparaiso, Rio Janeiro, or Para. But if not, then look out for a geographical division as far removed from these as possible."

On the other hand, to those investors who are still afraid of risking their capital in foreign countries, and will only consent to invest in their own, he has two pieces of advice to give. The first is that they can invest entirely in their own country "(1) if they will watch the variations of exports and imports; (2) the gold market; (3) the Board of Trade Returns; and (4) if they will realise their holdings during each cycle of prosperity, and wait for the cycle of depression to reinvest." His second piece of advice is addressed to the solid investor who makes the security of his capital his main object. He declares that the best substitute for Geographical Distribution is "(1) careful choice of varied local enterprises, with no two companies identical in their objects or trade interests; (2) all of them as far as possible removed from *general trade* fluctuations; (3) where the business is for the *general population*, and not for a few chosen individuals with whom the company does business."

With the above excellent advice we may now close our consideration of Mr. Lowenfeld's scheme of investment by the Geographical Distribution of Capital—a scheme which I can commend to the reader for its financial insight, penetration, originality, and, as I believe, essential truth. If not absolutely complete, other financial observers have now only to improve on it; but as a first and already well-tried scheme, and as developing, as Professor Brämer says, the "principles of a new science, Comparative Trade Statistics," it is beyond all praise.

I have neither experience nor authority to speak of the correctness or otherwise of its statistical details, but I agree entirely with its principles, and that frankly, because they run in harmony with my own system of Political Economy as embodied in my Wheel of Wealth.

www.ingramcontent.com/pod-product-compliance
Lightning Source LLC
Chambersburg PA
CBHW070822180526
45168CB00002B/718